The Strengths-Based Guide to Supporting Autistic Children

The Strengths-Based Guide to Supporting Autistic Children

A Positive Psychology Approach to Parenting

Claire O'Neill

Illustrated by Mary Foley

Jessica Kingsley Publishers
London and Philadelphia

First published in Great Britain in 2023 by Jessica Kingsley Publishers
An imprint of Hodder & Stoughton Ltd
An Hachette Company

1

To Eamonn, Cuan, Aifric, Mary and Ray. Thank you for being such a loving family. I am grateful for all your support and inspiration, especially while writing this book.

Contents

Preface

I wrote this book because I wanted to share the power of identifying, exploring and developing strengths for autistic individuals and in particular, autistic children. In my experience, being aware of one's strengths and using them effectively has the potential to vastly improve quality of life for an autistic individual. This book is written with autistic children and their families in mind, because the sooner we know the strengths of the child, the earlier we can get started on harnessing the potential of their strengths and, by so doing, enriching the lives of all involved in the process.

Knowing my signature character strengths would have helped me so much as an autistic child. Like too many autistic children, I spent my childhood feeling very different from others. I far preferred the company of adults, and nothing compared to the world of my imagination and the alternative universes of the books that I read voraciously. I was painfully shy and often did not talk, partly because of comments from others about my differences. As a child, I loved to gather facts on varied topics like gemstones, trees, dinosaurs and ancient civilizations. Facts and classifications were comforting and far less confusing than other children, who would call me weird on their kinder days. My parents were very supportive of me discovering new hobbies, so I was able to add crafts, ballet and swimming to my collection of interests. In addition to character strengths, my parents developed several family habits like walking and cycling that helped me develop a love of nature, and I have so many vivid memories of holidays spent outdoors on beaches, up mountains, in forests and by lakesides. While writing this description of my childhood pastimes, I can clearly identify strengths, such as curiosity, love of learning and appreciation of beauty and excellence. However, as a child, I had no idea of my strengths and was too painfully aware of what I saw as my weaknesses or failures. Being blind to my strengths added to a sense of struggle in my childhood. I can recall numerous times my classmates and I were asked to name our talents in school and I had nothing to say, which left leaving a burning sense of shame. My quiet, daydreamy and bookish ways were not noticeably valued or seen as strengths by me or my teachers. This difficulty with identifying my strengths continued throughout my adolescence and young adulthood, and throughout this period, masking and camouflaging hid my strengths even further.

Thankfully, by the time I became a teacher, I was more aware of my strengths. I was keenly aware of the importance of promoting the health and wellbeing of my pupils. As I moved into leadership roles in schools, I saw the importance of wellbeing for whole-school communities. My training in wellbeing, positive psychology, mindfulness and coaching gave me the skills to promote and support several wellbeing programmes in the schools I worked in. Being seconded from my teaching position to support schools as a Health and Wellbeing Advisor allowed me to help schools and their staff promote and foster health and wellbeing in pupils. Over the years, I have combined my training and experience to facilitate many wellbeing courses for both parents and teachers that advocate a strengths-based approach.

My journey has helped me develop a strengths-based approach with my own children. Family life is, without a doubt, a challenge at times for all of us living together as four neurodivergent individuals, all with our different needs and challenges. However, being strength-aware has brought many moments of joy to our family life. It is this potential for growth and joy that I now want to share in this book. It is my sincere hope that you enjoy reading this book and that you and your child benefit from the information it contains. I have loved using my strengths in writing this book. It is my wish that this book helps autistic children and their families to find fun and creative ways to identify, explore and use strengths both now and in the future.

PART ONE

Introduction

CHAPTER ONE

Introduction

I am so excited that you have decided to read this book. It is my hope that the book will convince you to take a strengths-based approach with your child. I have found that as an autistic individual, knowing about my character strengths and learning how to use them for my benefit has been invaluable in both my personal and professional life. I use a strengths-based approach with my own children, the children I teach and their families and many other autistic individuals. Over my many years of using strengths I have devised a framework called the IDEAS Framework that maximizes the potential of a character-strengths approach and I am so thrilled to be sharing this effective approach with you.

Who Is This Book For?

This book is written primarily for parents of autistic children and adolescents. For too long, a significant amount of the advice for parents of autistic children has been deficit-based, that is, a focus on what your child finds difficult and challenging. For certain, we have to support our children in areas that they find challenging and make environmental adaptations wherever necessary. However, focusing exclusively on weakness is detrimental to self-efficacy, self-worth and relationships. By focusing on strengths, you raise awareness of your child's positive traits and talents. This, in my experience, is a powerful and sometimes transformative approach. The information, resources and suggestions contained in this book may also be of interest to professionals who work with autistic children. Ultimately, the activities, although written with autistic children and their parents in mind, could potentially be used by anyone who has an interest in trying a character-strengths-based approach.

What Is in This Book?

This book is divided into three distinct sections. It is possible to start at the main body, but I do recommend reading the introductory chapters as they provide a context and useful background information.

Part One

Part One is comprised of an introduction and a chapter on the main ideas that are foundational to many of the activities and approaches outlined in the book.

Part Two

This is the main body of the book and contains a detailed exploration of the IDEAS Framework. Each component of the framework has its own chapter and resources.

Part Three

Part Three explores different ways of using a strengths-based approach, including using the IDEAS Framework for your own personal development. It also contains a chapter on how to use a strengths-based approach in advocacy and a conclusion to consolidate the information shared in this book.

All pages marked with ✳ can be downloaded from www.jkp.com/catalogue/book/9781839972157.

What Is a Strengths-Based Approach?

'Strengths-based approach' is a term that you are very likely to have heard, possibly in your child's school, in a book or at work. Even though many individuals and organizations try to operate from a strengths-based approach, it is not common to see individuals, professionals or institutions taking a strengths-based approach that has a firm foundation in the core values, standards, principles and overarching philosophy of a strengths-based approach (Hammond 2010).

I aim to be clear in what I mean by a strengths-based approach, and in this book, we focus on a subset of strengths, that is, character strengths. It is, however, important for us to have an understanding of the foundations of strengths-based approaches before focusing more intently on character strengths. A strengths-based approach does not ignore that individuals have challenges. Instead, in a strengths-based approach, a holistic view is taken of strengths and challenges so that the child is very well supported.

Problems with Taking a Challenges- or Deficit-Based Approach

- A deficit-based approach does not take a holistic view of the individual to include their unique strengths and talents.
- This approach often sees the 'problem' as being within the person and not due, or partially due, to external factors like stressful environments, unsuitable supports in school or lack of adequate resources.
- A deficit-based approach overfocuses on the challenges. This can be demotivating to the individual.

(Hammond 2010)

Advantages of a Strengths-Based Approach

- A strengths-based approach is a person-centred approach.
- With this approach, strengths are identified and valued.
- In a strengths-based approach, the individual's environment is considered, and adaptations are made where necessary.
- In this approach, other constraints are considered and efforts are made to remove them where possible.

(McCashen 2005)

Nine Principles of a Strengths-Based Approach
According to Hammond, there are nine principles that underpin a strengths-based approach:

- A belief that every child has potential, and it is their unique strengths and not their challenges that should be the focus of any intervention.
- What we focus on becomes the reality, therefore it is important to focus on strengths and see challenges as an opportunity to grow and learn.
- Language matters. The language we use to describe our children and their strengths and challenges creates reality.
- Change is inevitable in your child's life.
- Positive change occurs with strong and positive relationships; children need to know someone cares and will hold them in unconditional positive regard.
- A child's story is important. We need to start any change process with what is important to the child and their family, not the professional.
- Children have more confidence and comfort to try the unknown when they are empowered to start from what they already know.
- Capacity building is a process and a goal. Both the journey and the destination are important.
- Collaboration and respect for differences is essential for a strengths-based approach.

(Hammond 2010)

Why Take a Strengths-Based Approach with Your Autistic Child?

There are so many reasons to take a strengths-based approach with your autistic child, and I am confident that after reading this book, you will have more reasons to add to this list.

- You and your child have most likely had encounters with deficit approaches. The approach in this book is far more positive and uplifting.
- The strategies outlined are fun and positive, and you will discover the strategies that you and your child enjoy most.

- This approach fits in with a neurodiversity model of autism. Throughout the book, there is an understanding that autistic children may be different in some areas, but they are never less than neurotypical children.
- Your child, by engaging with the approaches in this book, will build transferable and lifelong skills.
- You will enhance your relationship with your child by engaging in the exercises in this book.
- Many of the exercises in this book have the potential to increase the self-efficacy and self-esteem of your child.
- Some of the activities in the book will lay the foundations for self-advocacy.
- I have seen this approach work with many children and adults.

Language Used in This Book

Language is a highly contested area in autism, and it is very important. When I facilitate autism workshops or go to autism-related meetings for my family, I state my language preferences. In this book, I use identity-based language, that is, *autistic children*. This is in direct contrast to the professional training I received where the advice was to use person-first language (IFL), that is, *child with autism*. Generally, the autistic community prefers identity-first language. As a general guideline, it is a good idea to ask the autistic person their language preferences. My language use in relation to autism is rooted in the neurodiversity movement, and, as such, I do not use functioning labels like high functioning, low functioning, mild autism or severe autism.

How to Use This Book

This book is designed to be used flexibly. You may be curious about a strengths-based approach, and it is fine to read the book from cover to cover without completing the activities. I think the book works best as a guidebook to be worked through slowly. I would recommend purchasing a notebook and possibly a scrapbook or another notebook for your child. These will be used as *strengths diaries*. After identifying your child's strengths, it is helpful to think of the suggestions in the book as a menu;

not all parts will be applicable to your child now but may be in time. You may decide to discover and explore your own character strengths first, and there is merit to this approach as it will support your own wellbeing, and modelling positive behaviours will benefit your child. If this is the case, Chapter Eight would be an ideal starting point.

The IDEAS Framework

The nucleus of this book is the IDEAS Framework. I developed this framework and have used it successfully in a wide range of settings. I know it has benefitted my parenting. I hope it will make the book easier to navigate by providing a map of the approaches and information you will be gathering as you use the book. The IDEAS Framework comprises of the following stages.

- *Identify* – You start by identifying your child's strengths, using a multipronged approach.
- *Describe* – The *Describe* section is where each of the character strengths are described thoroughly.
- *Explore* – The *Explore* chapter provides you with several suggestions that will make exploring your child's strengths a fun experience.
- *Action* – In the *Action* chapter, several strengths-developing activities are outlined with accompanying worksheets.
- *Support* – Finally, in the *Support* chapter, we explore ways to provide support for you and your child in using a character-strengths approach to benefit your child.

Throughout the book, I make references to my experiences as an autistic individual, a professional working with autistic people and a parent of autistic children. I hope this personalizes the book and lets you know that I am not writing about this topic from a removed position. I also hope that you enjoy reading and using this book and that it benefits both you and your child.

In Summary

▸ This brief introductory chapter acts as a signpost to the rest of the book.

▸ This chapter outlines who the book is for, the contents of the book, what is involved in a strengths-based approach, language, how to use the book and the IDEAS Framework.

▸ It highlights that the book is primarily written for parents of autistic children and teens and that it may also be of interest to professionals supporting autistic children and young people.

▸ It provides a detailed overview of what is meant by a strengths-based approach.

▸ It discusses language in relation to autism and explicitly outlines the rationale for the identity-first language used throughout the book.

▸ A brief explanation is given of the IDEAS Framework acronym.

CHAPTER TWO

The Foundations

Positive Psychology

Positive psychology is an exciting field of psychology that focuses on helping individuals flourish. Although a relatively new branch of psychology, it is underpinned by the works of the ancient philosophers and humanism. Two psychologists named Martin Seligman and Professor Mihaly Csikszentmihalyi (2000) wrote about the preoccupation in psychology with focusing on a deficit- and disease-based model of human functioning. They argued that this focus on deficit, disease and disorders has limited the field of psychology, and as a result, research and attention into optimal human flourishing has been side-lined by the discipline. Seligman and Csikszentmihalyi recognized that focusing on what is wrong will only get humans so far and they argued for more balance in the psychology profession. They started to investigate factors that would potentially improve wellbeing and lead to human flourishing.

So then, positive psychology in the simplest terms is the science of happiness and wellbeing. This progressive branch of psychology uses scientific methods to investigate and develop the positive aspects of our lives. In order to understand how positive psychology can help improve happiness, it is important to explore the concept of happiness. Broadly speaking, happiness can be broken down into two types: hedonic happiness and eudaimonic happiness. Hedonic happiness is concerned with pleasure and avoiding pain and hardship, whereas eudaimonic happiness is more closely aligned to achieving one's potential and finding meaning in life. It is positive to note that we can change our levels of happiness. Sheldon and Lyubomirsky (2007) outlined our levels of happiness as fifty percent genetically determined, ten percent based on life circumstances and forty percent driven by factors in our control. By using character strengths, we are actively using factors within our control to harness your child's potential for happiness.

The PERMA Model

Martin Seligman, who is sometimes called the father of positive psychology, developed a framework to help conceptualize and operationalize positive psychology (Seligman 2012). This framework is known as the PERMA Model. PERMA stands for positive emotions, engagement, relationships, meaning and accomplishment. Seligman and other positive psychologists developed interventions, known as positive psychology interventions (PPIs), that help individuals strengthen their PERMA. Licinio (2016) provides a comprehensive overview of the PERMA Model.

Positive Emotions

Positive emotions that have been studied extensively include joy, love, gratitude, hope, pride, inspiration, curiosity, amusement, serenity and awe (Fredrickson 2006). Fredrickson sees the role of positive emotions in helping us flourish, act and be creative. She calls this the Broaden and Build Theory (1998). Our genetics influence how we experience positive emotions, but we also have the potential to increase the amount of positive emotions that we experience in our lives. PPIs like savouring and visualizing can increase positive emotions. The term positive emotions implies that there are negative emotions; I am not comfortable with this concept and make an effort to teach my children that there are no negative emotions. Instead, I use the phrases comfortable and uncomfortable emotions. Positive psychology also recognizes that all emotions are valid and have a place.

RESEARCH AND POSITIVE EMOTIONS

- Increased positive emotions can benefit the individual physically, intellectually, socially and psychologically (Fredrickson *et al.* 2003).
- Positive emotions can mitigate against the effects of negative emotions (Garland *et al.* 2010) and help promote resilience (Tugade and Fredrickson 2004).

- Positive emotions protect against illness, including colds (Cohen *et al.* 2003), and stress and heart disease (Fredrickson and Levenson 1998).
- Positive emotions can predict a longer lifespan (Xu and Roberts 2010).

BUILDING POSITIVE EMOTIONS

- Start a regular gratitude practice. There are several ways to do this. I keep a gratitude journal and so does my daughter. We write and draw in these journals about things that we are grateful for.
- Taking time for hobbies or pastimes is effective in increasing positive emotions.
- Listening to uplifting music can increase joy and happiness.
- Exercise has proven benefits, including the increase of positive emotions.

Engagement

Engagement is linked to an important concept in positive psychology called flow. Engagement is also linked closely to strength use and development. Flow has been researched extensively by Mihaly Csikszentmihalyi. He discovered that a flow state happens when we are using our strengths to master a challenging activity. The key to achieving a flow state is to ensure that the level of challenge is just right.

RESEARCH AND ENGAGEMENT

- Being engaged in activities that use our character strengths increases physical and mental wellbeing (Linley *et al.* 2010).

BUILDING ENGAGEMENT

- Identify, use and develop your character strengths to increase engagement.
- Engage in activities that bring a state of flow.

- Try activities that have a mind-body connection like mindfulness, yoga or tai chi.
- Spend time in nature.

Relationships

Relationships are considered very important in positive psychology. We have relationships in many life domains including family, work and leisure. In a positive relationship, both parties should feel valued and supported.

Professor Shelly Gable is a leader in research into relationships and has developed a way to develop positive relationships called Active Constructive Responding (ACR). This approach teaches us how to react to and celebrate the good news of others. Instead of a lacklustre, 'Well done,' when your friend shares big news with you, Gable *et al.* (2018) advise that you respond actively with a comment like, 'I am so pleased that you shared this news with me. How did you feel when you heard the news yourself?' Being actively kind to others is another way of building positive relationships.

RESEARCH AND RELATIONSHIPS

- Work is likely to be more successful when colleagues are also friends (Harter, Schmidt and Keyes 2003).
- People who are with happy people are more likely to experience happiness (Fowler and Christakis 2008).

BUILDING RELATIONSHIPS

- Have some family traditions and routines like eating together where possible.
- Join a new club or a group.
- Meet the parents of your child's classmates.
- Get in touch with friends and family that you have not talked to in a while.

Meaning

Meaning is when an individual uses their values and strengths to contribute to society. It can make a person feel like they belong to something bigger than themselves and that they can bring value to society. Meaning requires effort and action. Having meaning in your life means something different for everyone. Individuals can achieve meaning through their family, work, advocacy groups, volunteering or being part of a church. Imagining their best future self can help an individual connect with a sense of meaning (Falecki, Leach and Green 2019).

RESEARCH AND MEANING

- Meaning is closely linked to purpose, and individuals who have purpose experience more longevity, better life satisfaction and fewer issues with health (McKnight and Kashdan 2009).
- Individuals who have meaning are more likely to have post-traumatic growth after an adverse life experience (Boniwell 2008).

BUILDING MEANING

- Spend time with family and friends who are important to you.
- Become involved with a group that is in some way actively good for society.
- Examine your strengths and values. Link them to what you really care about. Take some action based on this information.

Accomplishment

Accomplishment, also known as competence, achievement or mastery, is when an individual uses their strengths and efforts to achieve a goal (Seligman 2012).

Professor Angela Duckworth's research on a human quality known as 'grit' is central to accomplishment (Duckworth *et al.* 2007). Grit is closely linked to the character strength of perseverance. Perseverance is also linked to a growth mindset, where the individual has a strong sense of self-efficacy, that is, that with effort and determination, a person can achieve their goals. Goal-setting approaches, many of which will be explored in this book, are central to accomplishment.

RESEARCH AND ACCOMPLISHMENT

- Achieving goals increases our wellbeing (Brunstein 1993).
- Individuals who set goals that align with their personal values are more likely to achieve their goals (Sheldon and Houser-Marko 2001).

BUILDING ACCOMPLISHMENT

- Set yourself achievable goals – use the methods outlined in this book in Chapters Seven and Eight.
- Use the strengths you have used to achieve goals in the past to achieve goals in the future.
- Celebrate your achievements, both big and small.

PERMA is a wide-reaching wellbeing framework. It is not, however, without its critics. Criticism focuses on the individualistic nature of PERMA, the fact that it does not focus on physical health and that it overlooks cultural strengths. This has led some, including myself, to add other elements to the PERMA acronym. One popular addition is to add H to the end of the framework to include physical health. This addition is becoming more commonplace, with health being included in the PERMA(H) model in acknowledgement of the essential contribution physical health plays in general wellbeing. The addition is supported by research (Mutrie and Faulkner 2004, Faulkner, Hefferon and Mutrie 2015). There are some other very effective models of wellbeing that can be used with a strengths-based approach (Falecki *et al.* 2019). Indeed, I have used some of these frameworks very successfully with children and adolescents. I think it is worthwhile to look at some of these frameworks.

The Five Ways to Wellbeing (Marks 2008)

This is a very popular wellbeing framework with a strong evidence base. The framework has five components: connect, be active, take notice, keep learning and give. All of these components have been shown through research to considerably improve wellbeing (Marks 2008). These components are easier to explain to children than PERMA, and I have used this framework while taking a positive psychology approach with young autistic people.

The SEARCH Framework (Waters and Loton 2019)

This is a framework that I am really excited about, as I think it has huge potential in helping develop evidence-based and well-rounded wellbeing plans and interventions for autistic children and adolescents. Taking a strengths-based approach is one of the six pathways in the framework, so it is ideally suited to the topic of this book. The SEARCH Framework is an evidence-based framework that allows users to create actionable wellbeing plans that will have impact for children. The framework is very flexible and, although designed for researchers and educators, it is also of interest and use to parents. The six pathways of the framework are relationships, emotional management, attention and awareness, coping, habits and goals, and, of course, strengths.

Criticisms of Positive Psychology

There have been some criticisms of positive psychology. For example, Held in 2004 described positive psychology as being negative about negativity. The focus on the positive aspect of the human experience was seen as an unbalanced approach. This led to second-wave positive psychology, where the focus expanded from wellbeing to including a focus on the meaningful life and how qualities like grit and resilience are valued as part of the human experience. Now we are moving to a third wave of positive psychology, where practices like mindfulness and acceptance and commitment therapy (ACT) are part of the suite of PPIs available to aid human flourishing.

Positive Education

Even though this book is written with parents of autistic children in mind, I nevertheless think it is helpful to briefly mention positive education. Your child's school may take a positive-education approach, either as a whole-school approach or as an approach to wellbeing.

Positive education is the application of positive psychology in schools. The SEARCH Framework (Waters and Loton 2019) is a positive-education framework. Schools have been identified as significant environments in which positive-psychology interventions, like character strengths, can be identified and developed (Furlong, Gilman and Huebner 2014). Positive psychology, including strength development, can be used in so many different ways in educational settings, and it is critically important that autistic students are included in any positive-education interventions in their school. An organized approach to positive education that benefits all students, staff and wider school community is recommended (Green, Oades and Robinson 2012).

Positive Psychology and Autism

There is rising interest in using PPIs with autistic individuals. Indeed, positive psychology is seen as having significant potential to positively enhance quality-of-life outcomes for autistic individuals (Zager 2013). In a large study of autism articles, it was found that thirty-seven percent focused on the wellbeing of autistic people. Half of these articles focused on deficits and eleven percent focused on strengths. The remainder of the articles were mixed. The study ultimately recommends a strengths-based approach to enhance wellbeing of autistic individuals (Riosa *et al.* 2017). In another study, Dykshoorn and Cormier (2019) recommend blending positive psychology into autism research. This would mean a study of strengths through an autism lens, and, by doing this, researchers would arrive at a more balanced understanding of autism. This research would lead to a strengths-based, positive and balanced understanding of autistic individuals.

I have used PPIs with autistic individuals successfully both in a personal and professional capacity. There are interesting parallels between the emergence of positive psychology and the social model of disability movement. Both seek to shift focus from deficits and instead shine light on what is working well for individuals. The social model of disability puts a strong emphasis on personal interests and skills development. There is a need for more research into how positive psychology can be applied to helping autistic individuals flourish (Niemiec, Shogren and Wehmeyer 2017). A study that looked at how positive psychology could be used to assess autistic children saw that assessing strengths in the child and their family could improve interventions and help align outlooks of families and professionals working with the autistic child. This in turn was seen to potentially lower family stress and increase strengths of hope, perseverance and optimism (Cosden *et al.* 2006).

Character Strengths

The following list of VIA character strengths is central to this book and the approaches recommended throughout. VIA, originally an acronym for *values in action*, is a list consisting of 24 strengths found across different age groups, cultures and neurotypes. Throughout the book, this categorization of strengths will be explored in an in-depth manner. Any reader eager to explore VIA character strengths immediately can access information, including a free character strengths assessment, at www. viacharacter.org.

The Twenty-Four VIA Character Strengths[1]

Virtue of wisdom
Creativity, curiosity, judgement, love of learning, perspective.

Virtue of courage
Bravery, perseverance, honesty, zest.

Virtue of humanity
Love, kindness, social intelligence.

Virtue of justice
Teamwork, fairness, leadership.

Virtue of temperance
Forgiveness, humility, prudence, self-regulation.

---

[1]   List of twenty-four character strengths from Peterson, C. and Seligman, M. E. (2004) *Character Strengths and Virtues: A Handbook and Classification (Vol. 1)*. New York: Oxford University Press. Reproduced with permission of the Licensor through PLSclear.

Virtue of transcendence
Appreciation of beauty and excellence, gratitude, hope, humour, spirituality.

Before we take a deep dive into character strengths, let us look at the different types of strengths that we possess (Niemiec 2017).

Talents

Talents are things we naturally do well. To develop a talent to a high level, an individual needs to practise for thousands of hours. Howard Gardner researched talents in his *The Theory of Multiple Intelligences* (1983). Talents that are often attributed to autistic individuals include attention to detail and focus.

Skills and Learned Behaviours

Skills are what we train ourselves to do and learned behaviours are what we learn or are taught to do. In my experience, there is a significant emphasis on skill development when teaching autistic children. When we are skilled in something, we are said to have built a proficiency. Often, we learn a skill that others want us to perform rather than it being an innate trait within ourselves. When using skills, we can often be drained. This is in direct contrast to using our character strengths, where we are likely to be energized. For example, I have been described as highly organized, however, this is not a strength but a skill I have learned to manage my executive functioning (EF) difficulties.

Resources

These are best described as our external supports. For example, I would find it very difficult to write this book if I did not have the external support of an academic library. Resources is the only strength category that is external to us. Resources, as a category, is contentious in the context of autistic individuals. Too often resources like accommodations, removal of access barriers and support provision are in short supply and difficult to secure. Lack of necessary resources can often mean that autistic individuals are not reaching their full potential.

Values

Values are what we hold dear. They live very much in our head but guide our emotions and actions. Examples of values include freedom, loyalty, connection, respect, integrity and affection (Niemiec 2017).

Character Strengths

Character strengths can be seen as the driving force behind all the different strength types. They are considered the backbone of positive psychology. Martin Seligman and another positive psychologist named Christopher Peterson wanted to develop a classification guide for positive psychology, very much like the *Diagnostic and Statistical Manual of Mental Disorders Fifth Edition* (DSM-5, American Psychiatric Association 2013). This arose from a three-year project involving fifty-five scientists led by Peterson. The researchers met and debated the classification of strengths, using research, philosophy and religious traditions from around the world. This study helped develop a common language to discuss character strengths.

Niemiec (2017) explains the classification or hierarchy of the strengths very well. In Peterson and Seligman's 2004 work, the strengths followed a three-step hierarchical system. In this system, there are six virtues or families of strengths that are: wisdom, courage, humanity, justice, temperance and transcendence. These six virtues are followed by the twenty-four character strengths that we will be focusing on throughout the book. Finally, there is a description of situational themes where the strengths are used and expressed (Peterson and Seligman 2004). Niemiec creates further subdivisions in the strengths hierarchy. He places three virtues at the very top of the hierarchy, these being care, inquisitiveness and self-control. These are followed by the six virtues already outlined, and the six virtues are followed by the twenty-four character strengths. An important addition follows the character strengths, and this is context. Niemiec outlines the context in which strengths are used as being very important. Finally, the hierarchy of the classification ends with situational themes. For the purposes of this book, I will group the twenty-four strengths into their virtue families.

Linley, Woolston and Biswas-Diener (2009) offer a useful framework to assess if a personal trait is in fact a strength. They posit that a strength is a quality that:

- is pre-existing in an individual
- feels authentic to the individual
- energizes the individual
- promotes optimal functioning.

Character strengths are positive traits that are fulfilling to the individual and reflect that individual's personal identity. Our character strengths influence how we think, act and feel. Character strengths produce positive outcomes for both us and others. They are often expressed in constellations of strengths. We can have strengths in degrees, for example, lesser and signature strengths. Our strengths stay pretty stable, but we can develop and change our strengths over time.

For a positive trait to be classified as a strength, it must present in an individual across a range of acts, thoughts and emotions. The individual has to be able to use it in a range of settings. It must in some way contribute to what the Stoic philosophers and positive psychology refer to as the good life for the individual or others. There must be some kind of moral value attached to it. By using a strength, the individual does not diminish others; in fact, the strength often benefits others too. The strength must be in some way measurable. It must be distinct from the other character strengths (Peterson and Seligman 2004).

According to the VIA Survey, which is a means of identifying strengths, the most common strengths are kindness, gratitude, fairness and honesty. The least common strengths are self-regulation, prudence and humility. It is interesting to note that the character strengths most associated with wellbeing are love, hope, gratitude and zest.

Your top strengths are known as your signature strengths. They are usually the top three to seven strengths identified using the VIA Survey or other methods. For a strength to be considered a signature strength, a number of criteria must be met, including that using the strength must feel part of your identity and that the individual usually seeks out activities to use these strengths. It can often feel effortless to use your signature strengths, and a key feature of a signature strength is that the individual is energized by using it.

There are several reasons why we should focus on using our character strengths. The research tells us that if we are actively using and developing our character strengths, we are nine times more likely to be flourishing.

Furthermore, by using our character strengths, we are engaging with the PERMA Framework of wellbeing. Using our strengths helps counteract our negativity bias, that is, our tendency to focus on what is negative rather than what is positive in our lives. Using strengths has been shown to lower stress and depression, boost physical health and increase wellbeing.

There are a number of strengths classifications that are used in positive psychology. These include:

- the Values in Action (VIA) Survey (Park and Peterson 2009)
- the Centre for Applied Positive Psychology (CAPP Model) (Linley *et al.* 2009)
- the Talent-Based Strengths Model (Gallup Model) (Linley *et al.* 2009).

The VIA Model is the model I will use and refer to most frequently throughout the book. This model is based on Peterson and Seligman's 2004 classification and is therefore thoroughly researched and evidence based. It comprises of twenty-four strengths that are subcategorized by six virtues. The CAPP Model is another useful model that uses sixty strengths. It further divides the strengths into four subcategories. The strengths tend to be more relevant to a work or career environment. Finally, the Gallup Model uses thirty-four different talent themes and describes a strength as a well-developed talent. It will become clear throughout the book that there is no one ideal strength model and a multipronged approach to identification is the gold standard.

Your Child and Using Strengths

- Using strengths should feel natural, and your child should not have to put in a lot of effort to get positive results.
- Using weaknesses usually results in a lower performance.
- Persistently using weaknesses can bring uncomfortable feelings of anxiety and frustration, and a sense of failure.
- Even if your child puts in a great deal of effort into their weaknesses, their performance results are not likely to be as impressive as if they had put the efforts into their strengths.
- Completing a task when starting from a place of weakness is

likely to take much longer than a similar task started from a place of strength.

- More concentrated effort has to go into using weaknesses. This means your child is more likely to tire and have less energy for other activities.
- Your child can and will still achieve if using their weaknesses, but it is unlikely that they will want to repeat the process.
- If you encourage and empower your child to work with their strengths, they are more likely to succeed, which will lead to feelings of self-efficacy and pride, and a willingness to try the activity again.

Categorizing Character Strengths

Throughout the book, you will encounter different categories of strengths, signature strengths being the most commonly discussed. Niemiec (2017) gives a detailed account of strengths categories that I have adapted with permission here, and it is helpful to explore these categories before we start using the IDEAS Framework.

SIGNATURE STRENGTHS

Signature strengths are very important to the individual. They are directly related to who an individual is at their core. Using signature strengths is very energizing and often effortless. It is hugely beneficial that signature character strengths are recognized and positively framed for autistic individuals. Signature strengths is a phrase that you will encounter frequently throughout the book.

STRENGTHS ASSOCIATED WITH HAPPINESS

Many studies have identified several strengths that have an impact on happiness and life satisfaction. This is significant for autistic individuals, as numerous studies have shown that autistic individuals have lower life satisfaction and quality of life outcomes (Schmidt *et al.* 2015). Therefore, developing character strengths that have a positive impact on life satisfaction is very important for autistic individuals. Character strengths associated with life satisfaction and happiness include curiosity, gratitude, love, hope and zest.

LESSER OR LOWER STRENGTHS

These are strengths that are found at the bottom of the individual's strengths profile. They could be at the bottom of the profile for a number of reasons, for example, they could simply be undeveloped, undervalued or used less often than the other strengths. Sometimes, it is wise to consider developing lesser strengths, for example, developing strengths that are associated with life satisfaction or a strength needed to achieve a particular goal that the individual has set. Certain strengths like self-regulation are particularly important for autistic individuals to develop. Self-regulation is identified as one of my lesser strengths, but I expend energy every day using and developing this strength, as I know increased self-regulation will improve my wellbeing.

PHASIC STRENGTHS

This is where a strength is not a signature strength but it can be called on in a given situation as needed. In contrast to signature strengths, using phasic strengths may not leave the individual energized and may even drain the individual of energy. For example, bravery is a phasic strength in my strengths profile. I can be brave when a situation demands it, but using it is likely to leave me feeling drained of energy.

MIDDLE STRENGTHS

Middle strengths are very much like the middle notes of a perfume, as they enhance and support an individual's signature strengths.

LOST STRENGTHS

These are more likely to be found in adults. These are strengths that not only have not been encouraged and cultivated but may have been crushed by an authority figure. It is so important to value all of the twenty-four character strengths and find healthy and positive ways for children and adolescents to develop and express their unique strength profiles.

In Summary

▸ In this chapter, we explored the foundations of the IDEAS Framework.

▸ An overview of positive psychology was given to pave the way for strengths exploration.

▸ We investigated the PERMA Model and some other relevant wellbeing models.

▸ After this, we looked at some criticisms of the PERMA Model.

▸ Positive education was introduced.

▸ We delved into positive psychology as it relates to autism.

▸ We explored different types of strengths.

▸ We then looked at character strengths and categorized them.

PART TWO

The IDEAS Framework

Below are outlines of both the IDEAS Framework and the VIA character-strengths list. Both the framework and the list are key components of this book and are foundational to all recommendations and approaches shared. I developed and refined the IDEAS Framework over several years and I find it invaluable when engaging with strengths-based approaches like personal self-development, parenting, and supporting children, young people and adults as a teacher or coach.

I	Identify
D	Describe
E	Explore
A	Action
S	Support

Character Strengths for Children[1]

Virtue of wisdom

Creativity, curiosity, judgement, love of learning, perspective.

Virtue of courage

Bravery, perseverance, honesty, zest.

Virtue of humanity

Love, kindness, social intelligence.

Virtue of justice

Teamwork, fairness, leadership.

Virtue of temperance

Forgiveness, humility, prudence, self-regulation.

Virtue of transcendence

Appreciation of beauty and excellence, gratitude, hope, humour, spirituality.

---

[1] List of twenty-four character strengths from Peterson, C. and Seligman, M. E. (2004) *Character Strengths and Virtues: A Handbook and Classification (Vol. 1).* New York: Oxford University Press. Reproduced with permission of the Licensor through PLSclear.

CHAPTER THREE

Identify

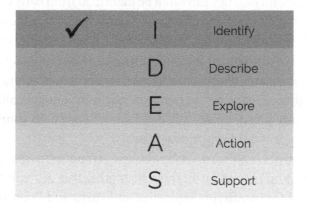

In this chapter, we will explore a wide range of strength-identification tools and methods. It is my hope that the identification of your child's strengths will be a positive and fun experience. I love to undertake the methods I describe in this chapter with my own children. It is an engaging and affirming process that demonstrates to me that they are maturing and developing. The methods that involve identifying strengths with your child are very positive in terms of relationship building. It is also uplifting to get the opinions of others that know your child and their unique strengths combination well.

This chapter provides you with simple and useable tools to identify signature character strengths in your child. This includes a checklist, illustrated strengths cards and a comprehensive description of the VIA strengths-identification tool for youth (from ten years of age).

Identifying Strengths in Your Child

Identifying character strengths in young people has preoccupied parents and educators across time and cultures. We have learned much about the identification of strengths, including that it is not a simple process. What we do know, however, is that character strengths are fluid and interconnected. Strengths present in individuals as a family of traits and are evident in the individual's thoughts, emotions and actions. Character strengths as outlined in the VIA strengths list are valued universally across cultures. They can be apparent to the individual and their acquaintances. They can often be identified from early childhood, however how character strengths present can change across the lifespan (Park and Peterson 2005, 2006). Park and Peterson (2005) advocate a broad blend of assessment methods, including self-reporting, observations and informants like parents, friends, family members and teachers. Self-reporting of character strengths can occur in younger children, but the VIA youth questionnaire was developed for use with young people from ten years of age for practical reasons.

The best place to start with taking a strengths-based approach with your child is to identify their strengths. It is difficult to advise one method for identifying strengths, and Parks and Peterson (2006) caution against using narrow identification methods for what is a wide and very individualistic field. Furthermore, when identifying strengths in autistic children, one should be mindful of several factors, including the child's development and communication style and preferences. Not every identification method included in this chapter will suit your child and many will require some adaptation. However, identification methods that are not suitable for your child now may become suitable in time. I have tried to include many methods to suit a range of ages, abilities and interests. Wherever possible, try to include the child as much as you can in this process.

Describing Your Child at Their Best

One informal but effective way to identify strengths is to describe your child at their best. When doing this activity, I find it helpful to have pens and paper or my strengths diary to hand.

Start by thinking of your child at their best. This may be on a particular day or during a particular activity that they enjoy. Try to recall this in as much detail as you can: your child's actions, utterances, body language and facial expressions and the keywords that come to mind as you recall this day or activity. Another way to record this is to represent your recall through drawing, mind mapping or spider diagrams. If you have a partner, consider doing this separately and comparing and discussing your recollections after the activity.

Next, look at the VIA strengths list and see if can you identify any strengths based on what you have drawn and written. Add your results to the My Strengths Table provided at the end of the chapter.

Strengths Spotting

Strengths spotting is a very useful exercise that can be done at different stages of the IDEAS Framework. To start spotting your child's strengths, pick a defined period of time of at least a week. Pay close attention to your child and try to spot strengths as they go about their daily activities. Do this at different times of the day, during different activities and with different people. Take note of what you spot. A variation on this method is to pre-record the strengths you think your child possesses and look for evidence over a period. If using this method, please keep an open mind! Dipping in and out of Chapter Four, *Describe*, can be useful at this identification stage, as it describes what each strength may look like in your child.

Ask the Experts on Your Child

Without a doubt, you and your child are the absolute experts when it comes to identifying your child's strengths. However, it is likely that there is a valuable team of experts that you can also ask to help in the identification of strengths. I would recommend asking siblings, grandparents, teachers and other adults who know your child well. I have often asked a range of people when identifying a child's character strengths. It can help to give the person a list of the VIA character strengths and ask them to mark your child's top-five strengths. It is also a very positive experience to do this as part of a conversation, as you are

41

more likely to get context and examples from the person you are asking. Use the My Strengths Table to record responses.

Ask the Real Expert – Your Child

There are many ways to identify strengths with the help of your child. The method you choose will depend on several factors, including your child's preferred means of communication, attention levels, and age and stage of development. With some children, a direct approach works best. For other children, an identification of strengths works best when approached from an angle. Your child may prefer to write or draw when identifying their strengths, and this should be encouraged. Depending on your child, it may be more beneficial to initially gather this information from others, like siblings, grandparents and significant adults in your child's life such as teachers, caregivers and therapists. You could also review the information gleaned from others with your child. This can be done at a later stage and can be a rich way to evaluate growth and progress.

Using Strengths Cards to Identify Your Child's Strengths

Strengths cards are a great way to start a conversation about strengths. I use these cards regularly with autistic children and adults, and they generate fruitful discussions in the identification stage of character-strength work. Strengths cards are visual cards that usually have a pictorial representation of the strength illustrated on one side. Often, the cards will name the strength and give a brief description of the strength on the other side. There is a simple set of cards at the end of this chapter. In my experience, it is often helpful to start with strengths cards rather than a list of character strengths, as they can generate powerful conversations. Certainly, I have never had the same conversation twice with these cards. I have found that using them with autistic children works very well, as autistic individuals often like having a third point or a focus point in conversations. In a conversation using these cards, the focus is on the cards rather than the individual, which tends to relieve a certain amount of pressure in social communication. You can also buy colourful cards that your child may enjoy, and I have given recommendations for these in the Further Reading section of the book. Initially, I tend not to display the name of the character strength with the illustration, as I find an untitled card leads to a wider and richer discussion.

Here are some tips on how to use the strengths cards to help you identify your child's strengths. I would typically do this over several sessions with a child, and this is very dependent on your child's level of interest, and attention and concentration levels.

1. Spread the cards out on the table.
2. Ask your child to choose a card.
3. Start a conversation based on the card.

Some questions you could ask:

- What is in the picture?
- What is happening in the picture?
- Tell me a story about the picture.
- Does the picture remind you of anything that happened to you?
- Does it remind you of any story we have read together?
- Does the picture remind you of any cartoons or movies we have watched together?

After some general conversations like this, you could then progress to attributing each illustration to a strength and sharing the simple description of the strength with your child. Based on this conversation, you could ask your child to pick three to five strengths that they think they possess. Ask your child to explain their choice to you. Note the strengths they have self-identified in the My Strengths Table.

Using Books, Cartoons and Movies to Identify Your Child's Strengths

This is one of my favourite ways to identify character strengths with children. Sometimes, children can find talking about themselves directly quite a difficult process, and talking initially about fictional characters is a gentle way to introduce the topic of character strengths. This is an identification method that works particularly well with autistic young people, who often have fine-grained knowledge about characters, especially in series like *Star Wars*, *Harry Potter* or *Pokémon*. There is a template to help with this exercise at the end of the chapter.

It can take some time to identify strengths in this way. While reading or watching a cartoon or a movie with your child, ask your child about characters and the strengths they possess. Ask your child what characters are similar and different to them and see if they can explain why. If your child is a fan of a character-rich series, you could identify character strengths using a mind map and the list of the twenty-four VIA character strengths as a guide. Add your child's responses to the My Strengths Table.

The Direct Approach – Using the List of Twenty-Four VIA Character Strengths with Your Child

Very often, a direct approach is what works best with autistic children and young people. One direct approach is using the list of twenty-four character strengths: ask your child to choose what they think are their top-five strengths. See if they can give reasons and examples for their selection. Record their answers in the My Strengths Table.

The VIA Classification of Strengths Youth Survey

The VIA Classification of Strengths Youth Survey is a free identification tool that is based on years of research with thousands of children and young people. This survey was initially developed by Parks and Peterson (2005), and it aims to act in a similar fashion to the DSM-5 (American Psychiatric Association 2013) but in a positive way: that is, to assess what is right with the individual. This was devised after a thorough examination of a wide range of literature concerned with youth development from diverse fields such as religion, ethics, education, childhood and youth development, philosophy, psychiatry and psychology. Each character strength had to meet strict and rigorous criteria before being included on the list of twenty-four character strengths. The creators caution that there is no quick method of assessing character strengths and ideally a range of methods should be used.

It is recommended for use with ten- to seventeen-year-olds, but I have administered it to younger children as part of a strengths-identification assessment. The survey contains ninety-six questions and takes approximately ten to fifteen minutes (longer if explaining questions) to complete. When using it with autistic children and young people, I find it is best to have an adult reading the questions, and explaining and clarifying when necessary. I find the conversation during the assessment is invariably valuable in getting to know the child better.

For a small fee, it is possible to receive a report based on your child's strengths. You and your child may like to have this, but it is not necessary. The report will provide a graph that visually represents your child's strengths, a research-based description of their top-five strengths, affirming adjectives that describe them as a person, information about under-used and lesser strengths and a guide for using their strengths. In my experience, this visually appealing report can add credibility to the strengths-identification process, particularly for adolescents. It can also be valuable evidence for school support plans and help students in self-advocacy efforts.

Pulling All the Information Together

By now, if you have been working through some of the identification activities in this chapter, you will have plenty of information to help you identify your child's strengths.

What I find helpful is to tally this information in the My Strengths Table. Add the source of the identification across the top of the table. Every time a strength is identified in your child, place a tick in the relevant box. A count of how many times each strength is ticked should give you your child's top strengths. Please remember that different strengths can develop over time, so it is worth reviewing identification of strengths annually.

Next Steps

Once you have identified your child's strengths, it is time to describe and explore their strengths in more detail.

In Summary

▶ Identifying strengths should be a positive and fun experience for your child.

▶ Identifying strengths should be a broad and varied endeavour.

▶ Different ways to identify strengths include:
   - using your own knowledge of your child
   - strength spotting
   - asking people who know your child
   - asking your child
   - using strengths cards
   - using characters from books, movies and cartoons
   - taking the VIA Classification of Strengths Youth Survey.

MY STRENGTHS TABLE

STRENGTH					
Creativity					
Curiosity					
Judgment					
Love of learning					
Perspective					
Bravery					
Perseverance					
Honesty					
Zest					
Love					
Kindness					
Social intelligence					
Teamwork					
Fairness					
Leadership					
Forgiveness					
Humility					
Prudence					
Self-regulation					
Appreciation of beauty and excellence					
Gratitude					
Hope					
Humour					
Spirituality					

MY STRENGTHS TABLE

Completed Example

STRENGTH	Describing your child at their best	Strength spotting	Child strengths cards	VIA	Feedback from: Granny	Tally
Creativity	✓	✓		✓	✓	4
Curiosity		✓	✓	✓	✓	4
Judgement						
Love of learning	✓			✓	✓	3
Perspective						
Bravery		✓			✓	2
Perseverance					✓	1
Honesty		✓			✓	2
Zest	✓		✓			2
Love			✓			1
Kindness			✓			1
Social intelligence						
Teamwork						
Fairness						
Leadership						
Forgiveness						
Humility						
Prudence						
Self-regulation						
Appreciation of beauty and excellence	✓	✓	✓	✓	✓	5
Gratitude		✓	✓		✓	3
Hope		✓	✓		✓	3
Humour	✓	✓	✓	✓	✓	5
Spirituality						

DRAW AN ILLUSTRATION TO GO WITH YOUR CHOSEN BOOK HERE:

Character Strengths in Fiction – Name of Book/Series:...............

Character strength	Character from book/series
Creativity	
Curiosity	
Judgement	
Love of learning	
Perspective	
Bravery	
Perseverance	
Honesty	
Zest	
Love	
Kindness	
Social intelligence	
Teamwork	
Fairness	
Leadership	
Forgiveness	
Humility	
Prudence	
Self-regulation	
Appreciation of beauty and excellence	
Gratitude	
Hope	
Humour	
Spirituality	

STRENGTHS CARDS

Cards are labelled with the number only. The strength titles with corresponding numbers are listed in Chapter Four, *Describe*.

5

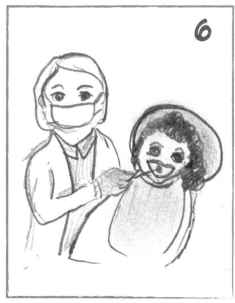

6

7

8

13

14

15

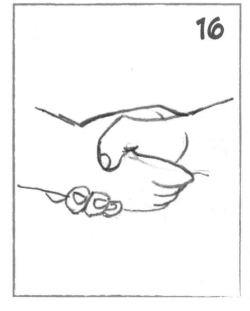

16

17

18

19

20

21

22

23

24

Describe

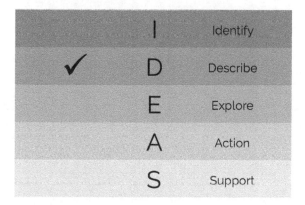

In this chapter, we describe the twenty-four-character strengths. Each strength is given its own section so that you can dip in and out of the strengths and read in any order that suits you. This chapter is the heart of the book and the one that I anticipate will be read most often. There is a consistent structure to each strength description, and I hope that this will make it easier for you to navigate the chapter. The character strengths are described under the following headings:

- Positive statement about the strength
- What is the strength?
- The strength and autism
- Why cultivate the strength?
- What the strength may look like in your child

The character strengths will also be given individual attention in Chapter Five, *Explore* and Chapter Six, *Action*.

Strength Family One – The Virtue of Wisdom Family

- Creativity
- Curiosity
- Judgement
- Love of learning
- Perspective

Character Strength 1 – Creativity

POSITIVE STATEMENTS ABOUT CREATIVITY

- I like to make new and useful things.
- I like to solve problems in new ways.
- I use my imagination often.
- I regularly brainstorm new ideas.
- I invent new games, words and characters.

(Peterson and Seligman 2004)

WHAT IS CREATIVITY?

Creativity is the production of original and adaptive ideas that usually make a positive contribution to the creator's life or the lives of others (Peterson and Seligman 2004). Creativity is both a process and a product.

CREATIVITY AND AUTISM

Quirici (2015) says that as a society we should question outdated and inaccurate stereotypes that autistic people lack creativity. In my experience of teaching autistic children, I have seen so much creativity that is expressed in wonderful and varied ways, like comic book creations, inventions, artwork and writing. Seymour and Wise's 2017 research centred on using circus activities with autistic children and found that the difference that the autistic neurotype brought to the activities fuelled creativity. The view that many autistic individuals have creativity as a signature character strength is supported by de Schipper *et al*.'s 2016 survey of autism experts where creative talents were viewed amongst these experts as a common characteristic in autistic individuals.

WHY CULTIVATE CREATIVITY?

The character strength of creativity can help the individual get into a flow state, which is very beneficial for wellbeing. Creativity is also associated with self-actualization, the desire to be the very best self that one can become.

WHAT CREATIVITY MAY LOOK LIKE IN YOUR CHILD

- Your child gets into flow states when involved in creative processes like making, inventing, writing and daydreaming.
- They may find novel ways for using and playing with everyday objects.
- Your child may often have original ideas or ways of looking at things.
- They may engage in the arts, like drama, music, poetry and visual arts.
- Your child may want to express their creativity in the way they dress or the way in which their room is decorated.
- They may play with toys in novel ways like making new creations from Lego™.
- Computer-based activities like coding and Minecraft can be very creative.

Character Strength 2 – Curiosity

POSITIVE STATEMENTS ABOUT CURIOSITY

- I am willing to try new foods and drinks.
- I am willing to try new experiences.
- I like to ask questions.
- I like to discover new facts about my interests.

(Peterson and Seligman 2004)

WHAT IS CURIOSITY?

Curiosity can be described as having a deep interest or desire for experience and knowledge. It is a desire to make sense of our world and experiences. Knowledge and learning fuel curiosity. Being curious is described as a positive and rewarding state. Everyone experiences curiosity to some extent, but we vary widely in how willing we are to experience it and have individual differences in terms of frequency and intensity of the experience of curiosity. It is interesting to note that curiosity is linked to anxiety, and we are enabled to be more curious when we are less anxious (Peterson and Seligman 2004).

CURIOSITY AND AUTISM

Neurodivergent people often experience the sensory environment differently to neurotypical individuals and can demonstrate a deep sense of curiosity about their environment. I have often experienced an autistic child taking delight in exploring their sensory environment, for example, a child exploring the movement of light and shadow with unabashed curiosity or comparing different textures with delight and glee. No doubt, I have also experienced the anxiety faced by autistic children with some sensory experiences, especially around food, clothing and noise.

In my experience with autistic children, I have seen curiosity expressed as an interest or a desire for knowledge many times. Barry Prizant, a researcher and writer, describes autistic curiosity as 'enthusiasms' and in his book *Uniquely Human* (Prizant and Fields-Meyer 2015), he recommends that we use curiosity or interests to engage with the autistic child to maximize learning and social engagement.

WHY CULTIVATE CURIOSITY?

Curiosity is linked to positive psychological and social outcomes. It helps children challenge stereotypes, fuels creativity and learning and alleviates stress and boredom (Peterson and Seligman 2004). Curiosity is also linked to self-esteem and wellbeing (Kashdan and Fincham 2002).

WHAT CURIOSITY MAY LOOK LIKE IN YOUR CHILD

- Your child may want to explore familiar and unfamiliar environments and sensory experiences.
- Your child may ask many questions and wonder about concepts.
- Your child may become very absorbed in the plot of a book or movie and be invested in what will happen next.
- They may enter a flow state while completing a puzzle, sudoku or crossword.
- Your child may watch with interest the movement of an animal or bird spotted in the back garden or on a walk.
- They may like meeting new people.
- Your child may like to examine interesting pictures and photographs.
- Your child is likely to think about the consequences of an event.
- They may listen carefully to the lyrics of a song.

- Your child searches for novelty.

(Peterson and Seligman 2004)

Character Strength 3 – Judgement

POSITIVE STATEMENTS ABOUT JUDGEMENT

- I can change what I believe when presented with new evidence.
- I can examine evidence when it goes against my beliefs.
- Changing one's mind can be a sign of strength.
- I use evidence to make decisions.
- I do not engage in groupthink.
- I am learning to be a critical thinker.

(Peterson and Seligman 2004)

WHAT IS JUDGEMENT?

A person who has the character strength of judgement has the ability to be open-minded and think critically. They can weigh up evidence in a fair manner. This is a character strength that is likely to develop with age (Peterson and Seligman 2004).

Individuals who score high on judgement think through scenarios, examine arguments from all sides, weigh up pros and cons carefully and do not jump to impulsive conclusions (Harzer and Ruch 2014).

JUDGEMENT AND AUTISM

In a study of autism and VIA character strengths, judgement (also known as open-mindedness) was ranked as one of the most frequent signature strengths found in autistic individuals (Kirchner, Ruch and Dziobek 2016). Furthermore, Attwood and Gray (1999) describe autistic individuals as loyal friends who speak their mind regardless of social context or strict adherence to personal beliefs, do not have ableist, sexist, ageist or culturalist biases and have an inherent need to seek the truth.

WHY CULTIVATE JUDGEMENT?

This is a highly desirable character strength. In particular, the cognitive flexibility required to use judgement is a useful life skill to cultivate.

WHAT JUDGEMENT MAY LOOK LIKE IN YOUR CHILD

- Your child accepts people for who they are rather than how they look or dress.
- Your child weighs up pros and cons carefully.
- Your child can identify two sides of an argument.
- Your child is loyal to their friends and family.
- Your child is unlikely to be a bystander in an unjust situation.

Character Strength 4 – Love of Learning

POSITIVE STATEMENTS ABOUT LOVE OF LEARNING

- I can't do this yet, but I think I will be able to do it in the future.
- I like to learn new things.
- I feel positive (content, happy) when I learn new things.
- I know a lot about...
- I like...
- I like to spend as much time as possible learning about...
- I know that if I try at... I can do it well.

(Peterson and Seligman 2004)

WHAT IS LOVE OF LEARNING?

Love of learning is a common top signature strength in autistic individuals (Kirchner *et al.* 2016). Indeed, it has been revealed as my top signature strength every time I have completed the VIA Survey over the years. It is certainly a very valuable strength to develop. In my work as a teacher, it is a joy to teach a pupil who loves learning. It is a character strength that I actively try to promote and develop in my two children. When we notice that a child has a love of learning, we can see that they are cognitively engaged and are experiencing positive emotions through the process of developing new skills and knowledge. By doing so, they satisfy curiosity, often build on existing knowledge and sometimes learn something new (Krapp and Fink 1992). Love of learning describes the way in which the child engages new learning and skills and also when a child engages with a well-developed individual interest. To experience love of learning, researchers suggest that the individual must feel a sense of competence and efficacy in the learning process. This may feel like building on previous knowledge, making connections between new and old knowledge or mastery of a skill (Peterson and Seligman 2004).

LOVE OF LEARNING AND AUTISM

This character strength can be linked to a trait that is common in autistic individuals called monotropism. This is a tunnelling of attention into a small number of enthusiasms or interests (Murray, Lesser and

Lawson 2005). Monotropism is linked to a range of educational and longer-term benefits for autistic children (Wood 2021).

WHY CULTIVATE LOVE OF LEARNING?

Possessing this character strength can help with motivation and cultivation of a growth mindset. If your child possesses love of learning as a character strength, they are more likely to persist in trying new tasks or engaging with new concepts until they are mastered. They are less likely to be motivated by extrinsic motivators like class tests and instead will learn for the intrinsic rewards gained in the learning process itself. Love of learning can rescue a person from feelings of boredom and repetition. It has important motivational consequences because it helps people persist through challenges, setbacks and negative feedback. Love of learning has also been associated with healthy, productive ageing (Peterson and Seligman 2004). Love of learning helps the individual learn that unwanted emotions are part of life, as the positive emotions of mastering new knowledge or skills are often intertwined with less welcome emotions of frustration while the learning process is active (Krapp and Fink 1992). Furthermore, love of learning leads to positive experiences, which may contribute to wellbeing (Csikszentmihalyi 1978).

WHAT LOVE OF LEARNING MAY LOOK LIKE IN YOUR CHILD

- Love of learning is closely linked to the character strength of curiosity. A child who asks questions about their world is likely to have a love of learning.
- Your child likes adding to existing knowledge.
- They will often demonstrate perseverance with new and challenging topics and/or skills.
- Your child may have a few favourite subjects in school.
- Your child engages in info-dumping. This is when an individual 'dumps' a copious amount of information during a conversation. Autistic individuals can find this very satisfying, particularly when they have a supportive conversation partner that understands that info-dumping can often be part of the autistic communication style.
- They may use love of learning to interact with others.

- Your child may exhibit a growth mindset.
- They possibly have a strong sense of self-efficacy when it comes to learning.
- Your child may become frustrated when learning is interrupted.

Character Strength 5 – Perspective

POSITIVE STATEMENTS ABOUT PERSPECTIVE

- I have self-knowledge.
- I bring both intuition and logic to decision-making.
- I have a wide perspective on issues and topics.
- I know the limits to my knowledge.
- I know my strengths and challenges.
- People ask me for advice.

(Peterson and Seligman 2004)

WHAT IS PERSPECTIVE?

Perspective is also known as wisdom or erudition. Perspective can be seen as a character trait possessed by wise people. When we think of people with perspective, we often think of older individuals like Yoda, the wise old woman in fairy tales or a grey-bearded magician like Albus Dumbledore. It is something more than intelligence, and the person with perspective has knowledge, judgement and the ability to offer sage advice. Perspective is used for the good of others and can both seek and provide answers to questions concerned with the meaning of life (Peterson and Seligman 2004).

PERSPECTIVE AND AUTISM

There is a need for research into the collective wisdom of autistic people and the benefits that their wisdom can bring to the autistic community. Many autistic advocates offer highly useful perspectives into what it means to be autistic. For example, the autistic psychologist, Maja Toudal, imparts valuable wisdom on how to manage one's energy as an autistic individual. Pete Wharmby, an autistic writer and teacher, uses social media to share his wisdom with the wider public on what it means to be autistic. Emily Lees, an autistic speech and language therapist, shares her perspective widely on how to support autistic children through the lens of the neurodiversity movement.

WHY CULTIVATE PERSPECTIVE?

A person with perspective is said to have expertise in the meaning of life (Baltes and Staudinger 2000). Is it said that a wise person knows how to plan and manage a meaningful life. Perspective is associated with positive ageing, physical and psychological wellbeing, and life satisfaction (Peterson and Seligman 2004). The most fertile window for perspective-related knowledge before adulthood is from about fifteen to twenty-five years of age (Pasupathi, Staudinger and Baltes 2001).

WHAT PERSPECTIVE MAY LOOK LIKE IN YOUR CHILD

- Your child is sometimes described as wise beyond their years or an old head on young shoulders.
- They can see the heart of an issue or a problem.
- Your child is likely to have insight into their behaviours.
- Your child is likely to be forthright and straight in their dealings with others.
- People seek advice from your child.
- Your child behaves ethically.

(Peterson and Seligman 2004)

Strength Family Two – The Virtue of Courage Family

- Bravery
- Perseverance
- Honesty
- Zest

Character Strength 6 – Bravery

POSITIVE STATEMENTS ABOUT BRAVERY

- I can try new experiences, even when they seem scary.
- I can face everyday challenges.
- It is okay to feel scared and ask for help.

(Peterson and Seligman 2004)

WHAT IS BRAVERY?

Bravery is when we use our judgement and act voluntarily, even when we are afraid in a threatening or frightening environment, usually to achieve some good. Being brave usually involves doing what is right; it is some sort of action towards a worthwhile end rather than risky action with no purpose (Peterson and Seligman 2004).

BRAVERY AND AUTISM

My experiences of being an autistic child and raising and teaching autistic children demonstrate to me how brave autistic children are daily.

Their sensory experiences are often confusing and unpredictable. They encounter neuronormative social expectations that are often daunting. Furthermore, they are often expected to carry out tasks that require a high level of EF that, depending on the demands of the day, they just may not have. These daily acts of bravery need to be acknowledged and valued.

WHY CULTIVATE BRAVERY?

Bravery is one of the most powerful character strengths you can support in your autistic child (Scarantino 2020). Bravery is linked to resilience. Resilience is the ability to bounce back after difficult experiences.

WHAT BRAVERY MAY LOOK LIKE IN YOUR CHILD

- Your child has the ability to engage in self-care, like visiting the dentist and hairdresser, even when it is challenging.
- They are able to plan for transitions, like moving into a new class or starting a new hobby.
- Your child is willing to try a new food. This can be so difficult for autistic individuals.
- Your child will ask a question in class.
- They are happy to speak to a new person.
- Your child stands up for what they believe is right and just.

Character Strength 7 – Perseverance

POSITIVE STATEMENTS ABOUT PERSEVERANCE

- When I fail at something, I am usually willing to try and try again.
- There is usually more than one way to solve a problem.
- I do not give up easily.
- I work hard and make my best effort.
- I can work hard towards a long-term goal.
- I brush myself off after setbacks.

(Peterson and Seligman 2004)

WHAT IS PERSEVERANCE?

Perseverance is when an individual voluntarily continues in the pursuit of a goal despite difficulties, obstacles and discouragement (Peterson and Seligman 2004). It is closely related to a trait known as grit.

PERSEVERANCE AND AUTISM

In a 2021 study, one hundred and fifty-three parents were asked to rate the 'best things' about their autistic children. Perseverance rated very highly in this study as children encountered the social and academic challenges of school (Cost *et al.* 2021). Another study explored how autistic students used character strengths like perseverance to achieve academic goals (Scott 2020).

WHY CULTIVATE PERSEVERANCE?

- Duckworth *et al.* (2007) expressed that the grit or perseverance a person has could determine if they will be able to complete long-term goals.
- Wolters and Hussain (2015) reinforced Duckworth's theory, explaining how, in education, grit is essential to outcomes such as students' engagement, achievement, retention and probability of graduation.
- Perseverance may help your child enjoy success more once it is attained.
- It improves your child's skills and resourcefulness.

- It can improve your child's sense of self-efficacy. This is the sense that one can achieve and accomplish goals and tasks.

WHAT PERSEVERANCE MAY LOOK LIKE IN YOUR CHILD

- Your child may find resourceful ways to solve problems.
- Your child may demonstrate a growth mindset and use phrases like, 'I don't know how to do this yet.'
- They may show task persistence and determination when a project becomes difficult.
- Your child may be willing to work hard over a prolonged period of time to reach a goal that is important to them.

Character Strength 8 – Honesty

POSITIVE STATEMENTS ABOUT HONESTY

- It is more important to stay true to myself than to be fake to be popular.
- Things will work out if I tell the truth.
- I would not lie to get something I want.
- I am honest about my feelings and opinions.
- I dislike when people are fake and dishonest.

(Peterson and Seligman 2004)

MASKING

Masking is a complex phenomenon common amongst autistic individuals. It is when the autistic individual masks or camouflages their true self. It is often done to avoid criticism and ridicule and/or to fit in with a social group. It can be conscious or unconscious.

Prolonged masking can be exhausting and is often detrimental to health and wellbeing. Accepting and celebrating who your child is as an individual is a proactive step towards limiting the effects of masking.

WHAT IS HONESTY?

Closely linked to integrity, authenticity and truthfulness, honesty is a highly valued character strength. Honesty is defined by factual truthfulness and sincerity, a character strength that we see when an individual lives close to their values and practises what they preach (Peterson and Seligman 2004).

HONESTY AND AUTISM

In 2015, two hundred and twenty-five autism experts were surveyed about autism, and honesty was identified as a personal characteristic commonly found in autistic people (de Schipper *et al.* 2016). Luke Beardon (2007), a well-respected autism writer, views honesty as one of the strengths widespread within the autism community.

WHY CULTIVATE HONESTY?

Honesty is associated with positive relationship outcomes (Deci and Ryan 2000, Scarnati 1997). Dishonesty is associated with low self-esteem and neutralization of guilt (Blankenship and Whitley 2000, Covey, Saladin and Killen 2001, McCabe 1992). Honesty and telling a trusted adult about uncomfortable incidents or feeling unsafe are important to stop abuse and bullying occurring and re-occurring.

WHAT HONESTY MAY LOOK LIKE IN YOUR CHILD

Honesty is a strength that is easy to spot, and it is not always easy to enact.

- Your child communicates what they mean and means what they communicate.
- Your child makes promises that they intend to keep.
- Your child tells you about their mistakes and actions, even when they know you will not be happy about them.
- Your child is true to themself.
- Perhaps your child's honesty can seem tactless or blunt at times.

Character Strength 9 – Zest

POSITIVE STATEMENTS ABOUT ZEST

- I am full of energy.
- I feel full of life.
- I feel awake and alert.

(Peterson and Seligman 2004)

WHAT IS ZEST?

A person with zest as a character strength is full of life, energy and spirit. Zest is seen as a desirable character strength and is associated with wellbeing. Psychologists have identified zest as a character strength that contributes strongly to life satisfaction (Bharath 2017).

ZEST AND AUTISM

There is very little information available in the existing literature or research in the area of zest and vitality in autism.

I find this very surprising, as in my experience of working with autistic children, zest is one of the most common character traits that I identify in these children. High energy levels sometimes have an adverse impact on areas like sleep, safety and learning, and it is prudent to support the child in these instances.

WHY CULTIVATE ZEST?

- Life seems fun for zestful individuals.
- A zestful person feels enthusiastic! This is an attractive quality to exhibit.
- An individual with the character strength of zest constantly wants to do things and explore.
- A person with zest feels more powerful and full of positivity!

WHAT ZEST MAY LOOK LIKE IN YOUR CHILD

- Your child may exhibit boundless energy.
- They don't tire easily.
- Your child's energy is sometimes infectious and spreads to others.

Strength Family Three – The Virtue of Humanity Family

- Love
- Kindness
- Social intelligence

Character Strength 10 – Love

POSITIVE STATEMENTS ABOUT LOVE

- There is someone that I can be my true self around.
- There is someone who I trust to care for and protect me, no matter what.
- There is someone I hate to be separated from.
- There is someone whose happiness I really care about.
- I feel physically affectionate towards this person.
- There is someone whose company I enjoy above most others.

(Peterson and Sellyman 2004)

WHAT IS LOVE?

Love is a stance composed of thoughts, emotions and behaviours towards another person. It comes in three broad forms:

1. Love for the individuals who love and care for us.
2. Love for the individuals we love and care for.
3. Romantic love.

(Peterson and Seligman 2004)

LOVE AND AUTISM

In a study of one hundred and fifty-three parents of autistic children, love was one of the top character strengths identified by parents in their children (Cost *et al.* 2021). This matches my experience, both personal and professional. Communication differences may mean that your child may not tell you that they love you. Sensory preferences may mean that your child does not like hugging. These differences do not mean that your child does not love you. Instead, your child may have unique ways to show you that you are loved.

WHY CULTIVATE LOVE?

Positive psychology studies link character strengths, especially those associated with social interactions (i.e. love and gratitude) or optimism (hope and zest), with higher levels of life satisfaction (Lavy and Littman-Ovadia 2011).

WHAT LOVE MAY LOOK LIKE IN YOUR CHILD

This will be individual to your child.

- They may enjoy sharing interests with you.
- Your child may value sharing special routines with you like bedtime stories and songs.
- Your child may seek out your company.
- They may tell you that they love you.
- Your child may demonstrate love through hugging.
- They may talk about you when you are not around.
- They may look for you when they are ill, injured or in discomfort.

Character Strength 11 – Kindness

POSITIVE STATEMENTS ABOUT KINDNESS

- I know that others are every bit as important as I am.
- Each and every human being is of equal worth. Being kind to others often brings them joy.
- It is important to give and receive.
- I am part of a common humanity.
- I try to give compassion and care to those who need it.

(Peterson and Seligman 2004)

WHAT IS KINDNESS?

Kindness is when someone is caring, compassionate and generous to another person or themselves. With kindness, there is a recognition of a common humanity where the other is worthy of attention and care for their own sake (Peterson and Seligman 2004).

KINDNESS AND AUTISM

Cost *et al.* (2021) conducted research that showed that kindness was a top parent-endorsed character strength in autistic children. At home and in school, I see numerous acts of kindness from autistic children. In my experience, specific praise that has a visual element is particularly effective in growing kindness in autistic children. Examples of this include 'caught being kind' displays or certificates or random act of kindness (RAK) displays.

WHY CULTIVATE KINDNESS?

- Kindness improves wellbeing and mental health (Taggart 2015).
- Being kind makes you happier (Otake *et al.* 2006).
- Volunteerism, which is closely linked to kindness, is linked to better mental and physical health (Van Willigen 2000).

WHAT KINDNESS MAY LOOK LIKE IN YOUR CHILD

- Your child shows compassion to themselves and others. This can take many forms, like soothing a sibling who has been injured or disappointed, or sharing a treat with a friend.
- Your child may give another family member a turn of the remote control.
- They may share toys on a playdate.
- Your child may give others turns with favoured toys.
- They may praise others and give them compliments.
- Your child may draw a picture for a sick relative or friend.

Character Strength 12 – Social Intelligence

POSITIVE STATEMENTS ABOUT SOCIAL INTELLIGENCE

- I can identify a wide range of emotions in myself.
- I know what causes these emotions most of the time.
- I can identify the emotional state of others.
- I can manage my emotions.
- I can act wisely in my relationships.

(Peterson and Seligman 2004)

WHAT IS SOCIAL INTELLIGENCE?

People who are said to be socially intelligent have a strong capacity to both experience emotions and strategize about emotion. They can recognize a wide range of emotions in themselves and understand their emotional relationships with others (Peterson and Seligman 2004).

SOCIAL INTELLIGENCE AND AUTISM

In my experience, there is a widespread core belief that autistic individuals lack social intelligence (Baron-Cohen *et al.* 1999, Torske *et al.* 2018). Indeed, social communication, which relies on social intelligence, is considered a core difficulty in autism and is part of the diagnostic criteria (American Psychiatric Association 2013). However, there is an increasing body of research that shows that social intelligence can be taught (Gilar-Corbí *et al.* 2018, Rezaei and Jeddi 2020). Furthermore, there has been an explosion of research based on Milton's Double Empathy Problem (2012). Milton's Double Empathy Theory suggests that there can be communication breakdowns in social interactions between autistic and non-autistic individuals. The reasons for this are complex, but differences in experiencing the world and different neurotypes play a part in this communication breakdown. This is relevant to social intelligence and autism, as Milton's theory makes us consider that difficulties in social communication are not the sole responsibility or fault of the autistic individual. This has significant implications for social-skills programmes that encourage autistic children to interact in ways that are not true to their neurotype or communication style. However, social communication is only one facet of social intelligence. An awareness of one's emotions is an important indicator of social intelligence. Two related areas can make recognizing emotions difficult for autistic individuals. These are alexithymia and interoception. Interoception is a sensory system that helps you feel what is going on inside your body. Feelings in our body are very closely linked to emotions. For example, a racing heartbeat may indicate love or fear. Many autistic individuals experience interoception differently, and this can have an impact on emotional awareness. Alexithymia is the name given when an individual has difficulty in describing and/or recognizing their emotions. It is linked closely to interoception.

WHY CULTIVATE SOCIAL INTELLIGENCE?

The character strength of social intelligence helps the individual to build strong relationships. In his 2012 book, Daniel Goleman outlines several compelling reasons to develop social intelligence. There is evidence to suggest that connecting with others strengthens our immune system, improves general wellbeing and reduces levels of stress.

WHAT SOCIAL INTELLIGENCE MAY LOOK LIKE IN YOUR CHILD

- Your child can accurately name a wide range of emotions in themselves, especially as they are experiencing them.
- Your child can manage and regulate their emotions.
- Your child can accurately name a wide range of emotions in others as they are experiencing them.
- They can influence the emotions of others, especially to reach a desired goal, for example, motivate a team to play better in a game.

Strength Family Four – The Virtue of Justice Family

- Teamwork
- Fairness
- Leadership

Character Strength 13 – Teamwork

POSITIVE STATEMENTS ABOUT TEAMWORK

- I like to work for the good of my team.
- I try my best to collaborate and cooperate with others in a team.
- I feel responsibility to make my home and neighbourhood a better place.
- I think it is important to help others.
- I care about the environment and would like to be involved in activities that help to keep it clean and safe.

(Peterson and Seligman 2004)

WHAT IS TEAMWORK?

The character strength of teamwork is concerned with the ability to be part of a group and work with teammates towards a common goal. It involves collaboration and cooperation. Teamwork is closely linked to citizenship, social responsibility and loyalty (Peterson and Seligman 2004).

TEAMWORK AND AUTISM

There is a wide range of research on teamwork and autism, but this research centres on the importance of taking a team approach to supporting autistic individuals (Dillenburger *et al.* 2014, Gebhardt *et al.* 2015). Visual schedules and pre-teaching of tasks and skills can help autistic individuals engage in meaningful teamwork (White *et al.* 2011). In my house, it certainly helps to have visual chore charts based on everyone's preferences and strengths. When building with Lego™, my family have clearly defined roles based on our strengths.

WHY CULTIVATE TEAMWORK?

The ability to work collaboratively and in cooperation is an important life skill to learn. In teamwork, core skills like turn-taking, winning and losing, helping others, relationship building and working with the strengths of individuals on the team are developed. These are all valuable skills that are worthy of cultivation.

- Your child is willing to plan activities collaboratively with friends and family members.
- Your child is aware of what strengths they can bring to a team.
- They may engage in activities to make where you live a better place (pick up rubbish, sweep leaves outside neighbours' houses).
- Your child may be a member of afterschool clubs.

Character Strength 14 – Fairness

POSITIVE STATEMENTS ABOUT FAIRNESS

- Everyone deserves their fair share.
- I do not cheat.
- I try to be kind to my friends, family and classmates.
- I try to respect everyone.
- I try to respect people who are different to me.
- Even if my friend says it is okay to do something, if it does not feel right to me, I will not do it.

(Peterson and Seligman 2004)

WHAT IS FAIRNESS?

As a teacher, I am told regularly that the character strength that children want to see in their teachers is fairness. Fairness comes from making a moral judgement about what is right and just in a situation. Fairness is underpinned by justice and care (Peterson and Seligman 2004).

FAIRNESS AND AUTISM

At autism trainings, I have learned numerous strategies over the years to teach autistic children to turn-take and win and lose in a fair fashion. Indeed, research indicates that it is worthwhile to prioritize the development of fairness in autistic children.

Hartley and Fisher (2018) studied sharing and fairness in autistic and non-autistic children and found that both autistic and non-autistic children preferred equality over self-interest when playing games. It is interesting that both groups of children mentioned fairness at similar levels. However, autistic children were found to have some difficulties in evaluating when others were being fair in games. Their study advocated explicit teaching of recognizing when someone is being unfair in a game. It is not enough to teach autistic children to be fair; we also need to empower them to recognize fair and unfair actions in others.

WHY CULTIVATE FAIRNESS?

There are many reasons to cultivate fairness. Colby and Damon (2010) note that living up to your own ideal of fairness is important for self-esteem development. As an autistic individual, your child is likely to need to self-advocate during the course of their life. Developing a sound sense of what is fair is a crucial strength in self-advocacy work.

WHAT FAIRNESS MAY LOOK LIKE IN YOUR CHILD

- A child who looks out for others is likely to be fair.
- Your child may notice and point out injustices.
- It may be that family decisions are questioned for fairness.
- Your child may become upset at injustices in play, books and movies.

Character Strength 15 – Leadership

POSITIVE STATEMENTS ABOUT LEADERSHIP

- I like to be in the role of group leader.
- I can make a plan and explain it to my group.
- I can motivate others.
- I can help others do their tasks.
- I am often the spokesperson for my group.
- I am good at giving others roles I know they will be good at in a group.
- I am beginning to advocate for myself.

(Peterson and Seligman 2004)

WHAT IS LEADERSHIP?

There are many opinions and definitions of leadership. In terms of it being a character strength, leadership is a quality an individual has that helps them influence, motivate and help others to work towards a collective goal (Peterson and Seligman 2004).

LEADERSHIP AND AUTISM

Ableism seems to be rife when it comes to autism and leadership. For example, in a Danish study of autistic leaders, both autistic leaders and followers were critical of each other's skills (Worsley 2020). However, there are several examples of strong and transformative autistic leaders in the autism community. Charlotte Valeur, an autistic board director, speaks publicly about the need for neurodivergent leaders on company boards. The type of leadership we frequently see in the autism community is advocacy. Self-advocacy is a legitimate form of leadership that supports others through example. Research shows that autistic people are far more likely to miss out on opportunities to develop leadership skills early in life (Purkis 2017). Therefore, we as parents and teachers should explore leadership with autistic children and nurture it when it presents as a character strength.

WHY CULTIVATE LEADERSHIP?

- Your autistic child may need to self-advocate for themselves with services, educational institutions and employers. Cultivating leadership skills will greatly help with this.
- As they grow and develop, your child may be in a position to mentor other neurodivergent children. Mentoring is a leadership skill.
- If your child is displaying leadership qualities, cultivating leadership will help them assume successful leadership roles in the future.

WHAT LEADERSHIP MAY LOOK LIKE IN YOUR CHILD

- Your child may be confident in voicing their opinion.
- They may frequently be the dominant one in play activities.
- Your child may be able to make plans, share them with others and motivate others to follow the plan through.

Strength Family Five – The Virtue of Temperance Family

- Forgiveness
- Humility
- Prudence
- Self-regulation

Character Strength 16 – Forgiveness

POSITIVE STATEMENTS ABOUT FORGIVENESS

- When someone does me harm like hurting my feelings or body, I can get over it quickly.
- I do not hold grudges for long.
- I do not try to seek revenge or get even with people.
- I think it is important to mend relationships when harm has been done.

(Peterson and Seligman 2004)

WHAT IS FORGIVENESS?

Forgiveness is when an individual's thoughts, emotions and behaviours have become more positive towards an individual or individuals who have done them harm (Peterson and Seligman 2004).

FORGIVENESS AND AUTISM

In a study of autistic children's capacity to forgive, it was found that autistic children did not take intent of the wrongdoer into account before forgiving (Rogé and Mullet 2011). Restorative practices (RP) are a set of approaches that help identify intent and so much more. This is an approach that I use with success with autistic children. RP are a set of values and a philosophy that use a suite of strategies to restore relationships when conflict or harm occurs (McCluskey *et al.* 2008). Here is not the place to go into detail about RP, but Burnett and Thorsborne include a 4F framework in their book that was developed by a group of Australian students and summarizes the restorative process very well.

The four Fs of the framework are 'fess up, face up, fix up and finished' (Burnett and Thorsborne 2015).

WHY CULTIVATE FORGIVENESS?

Forgiveness is linked to personal and societal wellbeing. For example, forgiving people have lower levels of anger, anxiety and depression (Peterson and Seligman 2004).

WHAT FORGIVENESS MAY LOOK LIKE IN YOUR CHILD

- Your child tends not to seek revenge or hold a grudge against those who cause them harm.
- They try to mend relationships with people who have hurt them in some way.

Character Strength 17 – Humility

POSITIVE STATEMENTS ABOUT HUMILITY

- I have an accurate sense of my abilities and achievements.
- I can own my mistakes.
- I am open to new ideas.
- I am willing to learn to do things better.

(Peterson and Seligman 2004)

WHAT IS HUMILITY?

Humility is a character strength that is in evidence when someone is unassuming about their abilities and achievements (Peterson and Seligman 2004). Humility has three aspects: an accurate representation of self; a modest presentation of self; an orientation towards others (Worthington *et al.* 2015).

HUMILITY AND AUTISM

During my research for this book, I searched in vain for any research or writing on humility in the context of autism. From my experience, I have seen humility expressed as a character strength in autistic individuals. In my class, I try to support my pupils to use their strengths to help others, and this helps cultivate humility.

WHY CULTIVATE HUMILITY?

One may wonder why we would consider cultivating humility when there is so much attention given to raising self-esteem. However, one can be humble and have high self-esteem. Humility is an often-misunderstood character strength and is sometimes thought of as a state of poor self-esteem and an inclination to self-deprecate (Hill and Sandage 2016). Humility seems worthy of cultivation, however, when we view it as a willingness to see oneself accurately, an ability to focus on the strengths of others rather than oneself and a desire to learn from others (Owens, Johnson and Mitchell 2013).

WHAT HUMILITY MAY LOOK LIKE IN YOUR CHILD

- Your child has an accurate estimation of their strengths and abilities.
- They can acknowledge their mistakes, challenges and what they still need to learn.
- Your child focuses on the strengths and achievements of others.
- People who know your child describe them as modest and humble.

Character Strength 18 – Prudence

POSITIVE STATEMENTS ABOUT PRUDENCE

- I care about and think about my future.
- I take time to think about the choices I make in life.
- I think carefully before making decisions.
- I see the big picture and can resist when I am tempted by poor choices.

(Peterson and Seligman 2004)

WHAT IS PRUDENCE?

Prudence is a character strength where the individual looks towards the future and uses reasoning, planning and self-management to reach their long-term goals. Prudent individuals have a balanced, flexible and moderate approach to life. Prudence is not characterized by undue caution, excessive self-restraint or strict conformity. It is a balanced, organized and proactive approach towards achieving future goals (Peterson and Seligman 2004).

PRUDENCE AND AUTISM

A prudent approach is supported by strong EF skills. EF is an umbrella term for a set of skills that are associated with the functions of the prefrontal cortex of the brain. These interrelated skills help the individual use and organize their thoughts, feelings or behaviours with their goals. Research indicates that EF difficulties are common in autistic individuals (Lemon *et al.* 2011, Memisevic and Pasalic 2021, Van Eylen *et al.* 2015). Certainly, as an autistic individual, I employ a wide range of strategies to support my EF. Supporting the EF of my own children and the children I teach is a priority for me.

WHY CULTIVATE PRUDENCE?

There is a link between prudence and psychological wellbeing. It is associated with positive characteristics like warmth, optimism, assertiveness, imagination and curiosity (Peterson and Seligman 2004). In terms of autism and prudence, cultivating and supporting EF skills may contribute to supporting a more prudent approach to life.

WHAT PRUDENCE MAY LOOK LIKE IN YOUR CHILD

- Your child may use a wide range of EF support strategies that help them reach long-term goals.
- They might be very future-orientated and make short-term sacrifices to reach future goals.
- Your child may think of everyday choices in a very practical and methodical fashion.

Character Strength 19 – Self-Regulation

POSITIVE STATEMENTS ABOUT SELF-REGULATION

- I can match my levels of arousal to the current situation.

- I can manage my emotions.
- I can manage my actions and impulses.
- I can override my initial response.
- I can often resist temptation.

(Peterson and Seligman 2004)

WHAT IS SELF-REGULATION?

Self-regulation is a character strength that is linked to an individual's neurological stress-response system. It is the ability of an individual to screen, gauge and modify their emotions and levels of arousal in order to function well, and behave and act appropriately in a given situation (Laurent and Gorman 2018).

SELF-REGULATION AND AUTISM

As an autistic individual, I expend significant energy self-regulating. It is a skill that I strive to help my own children and pupils develop. I have been very fortunate to train and work alongside talented occupational therapists who have helped me develop strategies to use personally, at home with my family and at school with my pupils. I have designed and facilitated self-regulation workshops for both school staff and parents. In my experience, it is a core character strength and is worthy of attention and development. Difficulties with emotional regulation are often a primary reason for seeking support for autistic children. There is little research into the crucial influence of parents on the emotional self-regulation of autistic children (Laurent and Gorman 2018). In the development of self-regulation, one can take a bottom-up approach, that is, using the body, senses and breath to aid regulation, a top-down approach, using cognitive strategies, or a combined approach. In my experience, I have found using a bottom-up approach initially and working towards a combined approach is most effective. In autism research, contemplative practices that work through both body and mind have shown some promising results (Tanksale *et al.* 2021).

WHY CULTIVATE SELF-REGULATION?

Emotional self-regulation has been linked to positive social-emotional development in early childhood and to pro-social engagement, social competence and desirable academic outcomes in later childhood (Laurent and Gorman 2018).

WHAT SELF-REGULATION MAY LOOK LIKE IN YOUR CHILD

- Your child can name a wide range of emotions as they are experiencing them.
- They may seek your support to regulate.
- They may use a bottom-up, top-down or combined approach to regulation.
- They may use deep breathing to regulate.
- They may use sensory supports like sipping, chewing, tugging and movement to regulate.
- They may stim.
- Your child may stop and think before acting.

Strength Family Six – The Virtue of Transcendence Family

- Appreciation of beauty and excellence
- Gratitude
- Hope
- Humour
- Spirituality

Character Strength 20 – Appreciation of Beauty and Excellence

POSITIVE STATEMENTS ABOUT APPRECIATION OF BEAUTY AND EXCELLENCE

- I often experience wonder and awe in nature.
- I find joy in physical beauty, skills and talents and the good deeds of others.
- I appreciate beautiful music and art.
- I admire people who demonstrate goodness and kindness.

(Peterson and Seligman 2004)

WHAT IS APPRECIATION OF BEAUTY AND EXCELLENCE?

This character strength is the ability to discover, identify and find pleasure in what is good in the physical and social world (Peterson and Seligman 2004). To date, it is one of the least-studied character strengths (Martínez-Martí, Hernández-Lloreda and Avia 2016).

APPRECIATION OF BEAUTY AND EXCELLENCE AND AUTISM

There is very little research done on this area. Cost *et al.* (2021) report appreciation of beauty and excellence as one of the least common traits in non-autistic or autistic children. However, I often identify appreciation of beauty and excellence in my own children and the autistic children that I teach. I am fortunate to be able to take my autistic pupils for a nature walk every day. Some of the children delight in nature and have a profound appreciation for flowers, birdsong, dew-soaked spider webs, frost patterns and the passing clouds. Other children that I teach appreciate the beauty of music, so much so that they can jump and dance in delight when they hear music that they really like.

WHY CULTIVATE APPRECIATION OF BEAUTY AND EXCELLENCE?

It is likely that individuals who possess this character strength experience more joy in life. Appreciation of beauty and excellence is associated with being open to new experiences (Peterson and Seligman 2004). Furthermore, the character strength is strongly associated with wellbeing. Individuals who have appreciation of excellence and beauty as a signature character strength are likely to have a meaningful relationship with nature and the Universe. They tend to be concerned for the wellbeing of others and have a belief in the genuineness of other people. Furthermore, individuals who have this character strength are less materialistic and less envious. Not surprisingly, they experience greater life satisfaction and tend to be less anxious (Martínez-Martí *et al.* 2016).

WHAT APPRECIATION OF BEAUTY AND EXCELLENCE
MAY LOOK LIKE IN YOUR CHILD

There are physical signs that may indicate appreciation of beauty and excellence, and these include goosebumps, having the mouth and eyes wide open in awe and tears (Peterson and Seligman 2004).

Character Strength 21 – Gratitude

POSITIVE STATEMENTS ABOUT GRATITUDE

- It is important to appreciate special moments in each day.
- I think it is important to give thanks and express gratitude to people who help me and are kind to me.
- I am often struck by the beauty of nature, and I am grateful for it.
- I see the acts of kindness of others as gifts to be grateful for.
- I am thankful for my family and friends.

(Peterson and Seligman 2004)

WHAT IS GRATITUDE?

Gratitude is a character strength that comes from a feeling of thankfulness and joy in receiving some beneficial action from another person. It is an emotion that can be felt as a thankfulness for life and nature.

GRATITUDE AND AUTISM

I try to cultivate an attitude of gratitude in myself, my children and the children I teach. It is also a character strength and emotion that I try to cultivate in the autistic adults that I support. Ideally, I do this by encouraging the individual I am supporting to keep a gratitude diary, but in my experience of working with autistic children, keeping a regular gratitude diary is something that must be built up to and needs some support along the way.

WHY CULTIVATE GRATITUDE?

Gratitude is not only a character strength, but it is also one of the positive emotions that Fredrickson (2001) identified that play an important role in the wellbeing of the individual. These positive emotions ready the individual's mind for learning, generate creativity and help build resilience. Fredrickson's 2001 Broaden and Build Theory provides a framework to explain how positive emotions have both an immediate and long-term effect on the individual's sense of wellbeing, health and happiness. There is scientific evidence showing that gratitude changes brain chemistry, which leads to enhanced wellbeing by shifting attention away from less comfortable emotions like envy and anger (Brown and Wong 2017).

WHAT GRATITUDE MAY LOOK LIKE IN YOUR CHILD

- Your child notices small and ordinary things to be grateful for every day.
- As your child's character strength of gratitude grows, they may be grateful for gestures of care and kindness more than material possessions.

Character Strength 22 – Hope

POSITIVE STATEMENTS ABOUT HOPE

- I think I am doing well in life.
- I am doing just as well as other children my age.
- If I have a problem, there is more than one way to solve it.
- I can keep going longer than others at solving a problem.

(Valle, Huebner and Suldo 2004)

- Despite having some challenges, I stay hopeful about the future.
- I look on the bright side of a situation.
- I can visualize my future.
- I learn from setbacks and know that they will help me do better in the future.

(Peterson and Seligman 2004)

WHAT IS HOPE?

Hope is when our thoughts, emotions and motivation are attuned positively towards the future. Hope is linked to optimism and a general orientation to the future (Peterson and Seligman 2004).

Santos and Groves (2021) describe hopeful individuals as persons who believe that they can find the means to achieve their goals and have the motivation and self-efficacy to follow the means or pathway to reach their goals.

HOPE AND AUTISM

There is very little research into the nurturing of hope as a character trait in autistic children. Research in the area of autism and hope instead focuses on fostering hope in the parents of autistic children (Birmingham 2010, Ekas, Pruitt and McKay 2016, Salimi *et al.* 2017). In my experience, hope is a crucial character strength to develop in autistic children. It can help with transition planning and managing change like moving to a new class or transition from primary to secondary school. Explicitly teaching how to plan and problem solve allows autistic children to experience and develop hope.

WHY CULTIVATE HOPE?

- Children who are hopeful are happier and experience more life satisfaction (Coulson 2021).
- Children who have the character strength of hope have more positive relationships (Coulson 2021).
- Hope is associated with lower levels of anxiety and depression (Peterson and Seligman 2004).

WHAT HOPE MAY LOOK LIKE IN YOUR CHILD

- Even when faced with difficulties and challenges, your child has a sense of hope about their future.
- Your child takes a solution-focused approach to problems.
- Your child makes plans.
- They have a sense of what they would like to do in the future.
- Your child expects the best outcome from every situation.

Character Strength 23 – Humour

POSITIVE STATEMENTS ABOUT HUMOUR

- I can often joke and laugh.
- I see the funny side of things.
- My friends and family say I am fun to be with.
- I like to brighten up the day with laughter.
- When my friends and family are sad, I try to be playful and/or see the light side of things.

(Peterson and Seligman 2004)

WHAT IS HUMOUR?

Humour may be a character strength that is easy to recognize but harder to define. Humour can involve playfulness, a cheerful view even when things are tough and/or an ability to make oneself and others smile and laugh (Peterson and Seligman 2004).

In my experience, it is a character strength that is a joy to be around. Humour is a character strength that I have observed often in my autistic pupils, and it takes many forms. My two children both have humour as a signature strength, and it is expressed very differently in both. My son's strength is expressed through his puns and witty wordplay that leave him and sometimes the rest of the family in mirthful laughter. My daughter has a mischievous sense of humour and revels in slapstick.

HUMOUR AND AUTISM

At autism trainings, especially language and communication trainings, I often hear that autistic individuals may find it difficult to use or understand sarcasm. This is a view also present in the research around autism and humour (Agius and Levey 2019). Instead of seeing this as a weakness, research shows that the appreciation of sarcasm is associated with bad moods (Ruch 2001). Humour has been successfully used as a behavioural intervention to reduce anxiety and stress, as well as for educational purposes in autistic individuals (Lyons and Fitzgerald 2004).

WHY CULTIVATE HUMOUR?

Humour is an important facet of everyday life. We use humour to form relationships and boost mood and as a buffer against stress (Dowling 2014, Ruch and Köhler 1998). It can increase physical health and even longevity (Martin 2007). The character strength of humour is socially desirable and helps forge social connections.

WHAT HUMOUR MAY LOOK LIKE IN YOUR CHILD

- Humour is a character strength that is easy to spot and often positive to be around.
- A child with the character strength of humour may find everyday situations that are not apparently humorous to others amusing.
- Your child may invent jokes, puns and riddles.
- Your child may especially like humorous cartoons, movies, books and joke books.
- They may like sharing their humour with others and appreciate when others use humour.
- Your child makes funny facial expressions designed to convey and share humour.

Character Strength 24 – Spirituality

POSITIVE STATEMENTS ABOUT SPIRITUALITY

- I like to pray.
- I like to meditate.
- I believe there is a sacred force in all living things and this force connects us.
- I believe that life has a purpose.
- I look to God or a Higher Power for strength and support.
- God or a Higher Power helps me understand my life and my experiences.

(Peterson and Seligman 2004)

WHAT IS SPIRITUALITY?

Spirituality is an awareness and belief in the transcendent. It is concerned with the meaning of life and an awareness and appreciation of our interconnectedness with other people, nature and the Universe. It may or may not involve a relationship with God and religion.

SPIRITUALITY AND AUTISM

In her research into autism and spirituality, Olga Bogdashina (2013) discovered that spirituality plays an important role in the lives of many autistic people. She explored how spirituality is experienced differently by autistic people and how it helps many autistic people find meaning in their lives. The spiritual needs and expressions of autistic individuals need more attention in research (Hills, Clapton and Dorsett 2019).

WHY CULTIVATE SPIRITUALITY?

- There is considerable evidence of the links between health and spirituality (Lewis 2009).
- Spirituality positively influences wellbeing and gives life meaning and value (Testoni *et al.* 2019).

WHAT SPIRITUALITY MAY LOOK LIKE IN YOUR CHILD

- Your child may have a sense of wonder about the world.
- Your child may believe in God or a Higher Power.
- They may like faith stories and parables.
- Your child may think about how God or a Higher Power might help them and others
- They may want to take part in rituals associated with their spirituality or religion.

In Summary

▶ This chapter covers the *Describe* component of the IDEAS Framework.
▶ It is intended to be a key reference and resource for the reader.
▶ As a key chapter in the book, it is, unsurprisingly, the longest chapter.
▶ Each of the 24 VIA character strengths is discussed following a similar framework.

CHAPTER FIVE

Explore

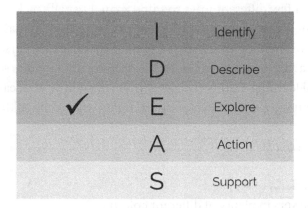

Once you and your child have worked through the identify stage of the IDEAS Framework, the next stage is to explore their strengths so that they can start to use and develop them to their maximum potential. In this chapter, I outline a few ways to explore strengths that lead to a deeper understanding of how each strength manifests in your child.

Mind Maps®[1]

Mind Maps® or mind mapping is a graphic-organizer tool and approach developed by Tony Buzan that can help individuals in several different ways. When using mind maps, we use different parts of the brain by drawing colourful pictures with key words that help us use memory and associations. In my experience, mind mapping is a very helpful method to use with autistic individuals. It can certainly help with EF skills like

---

[1] This section was inspired by Buzan, T. (2005) 'Mind Maps for Kids.' London: Thorsons, by permission of HarperCollins Publishers Ltd © Tony Buzan, 2005.

task initiation, organizing thoughts, planning and memory. Importantly, children generally like the mind-mapping process and it teaches them a skill and a process that can help them across the lifespan. Software is available that enables the user to create digital mind maps, and this software is often recommended by occupational therapists, speech and language therapists and psychologists when writing reports for autistic learners.

How to mind map

There are a few different ways to mind map. I usually pick the theme *myself* when teaching the mind-mapping method. Usually, when teaching this method to an autistic pupil, I subdivide the *myself* theme into several different categories, as I find this really supports social and emotional learning. I think the *myself* theme would be an ideal starting point if you were to start exploring strengths with your child.

MATERIALS NEEDED

- Blank A4 or A3 page.
- Markers in plenty of different colours.
- It is nice to draw illustrations, but some children and young people love using photos, printed images from the internet or cut-out images from magazines.

METHOD

1. Place the sheet of paper sideways at a landscape orientation.
2. Draw a picture at the centre of the page. For the theme of *myself,* a simple body outline is ideal. Alternatively, a photograph of your child would work well here too.
3. Write *myself* under, over or in the body outline. This is the main idea of your mind map.
4. Choose the subcategory you are going to mind map first. Some suggestions include:
   - physical appearance
   - my senses
   - my emotions

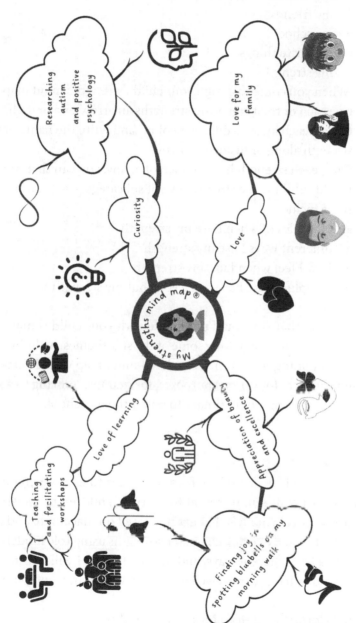

Example of a Partially Completed mind map

- my family
- my hobbies
- my friends
- my school
- favourite things
- my strengths.

5. When you come to design your child's strengths mind map, give each of their signature strengths an arrow or a branch. Colour each arrow a different colour and write the name of the strength along or inside the arrow.

6. Once each strength has a branch or arrow, you can then start to add sub-branches that represent subcategories. Examples of these include:
    - examples of when I use my strength
    - different ways I use my strength
    - how I feel when I use my strength
    - compliments I have received about my strength.

A great project that you could undertake with your child is making a myself-themed mind map using some of the sub-themes, including the strengths. A photograph of the completed mind map would certainly be a useful artefact for various purposes, for example, moving to a new class or transitioning from primary to post-primary school.

Role Models

Using role models is one of my favourite ways to explore character strengths with children. It is vital for autistic children to see strong neurodivergent role models that are not based on inaccurate and out-dated stereotypes. Exploring character strengths using role models can be done in a few different ways, and in this chapter, I will outline two approaches that have worked well with my own children and pupils.

Personal Heroes and Role Models That Share a Character Strength with Your Child

These are enjoyable ways to explore your child's character strengths. It can be very affirming to learn about a person who shares some of your personal traits and how this individual has used these traits to succeed in some aspect of life.

One way of using role models to explore character strengths with your child is to use role models or personal heroes that already influence your child. You could use the mind-mapping method outlined earlier, explore the character strengths that this personal hero possesses and look at how the individual has used these strengths for their benefit and for the benefit of others. Your child may well admire historical and/ or fictional role models, and these are all worthy of exploration from a character-strengths perspective.

Another approach is to explore a role model that is associated with a particular character strength. I have listed a suggested role model for each character strength. Most of the role models are neurodivergent. However, I think it is important to explore role models of all neurotypes with your child. Please do expand on my list and use role models that are known to your child too. It is important for your child to learn that you do not have to be famous to be a role model or personal hero.

Role Models by Character Strength

These role models possess more strengths than the one they are assigned in this list. Please highlight other strengths they may possess, especially if your child has an interest in the individual.

Creativity – Cara Delevingne is neurodivergent and uses her character strength of creativity in acting, modelling, writing and music.

Curiosity – Daisy Shearer is an autistic physics postgraduate researcher and experimental quantum physicist who uses her curiosity to explore science.

Judgement – Haley Moss is autistic and uses her character strength of judgement in her role as a lawyer and advocate.

Love of learning – Carl Sagan was a well-regarded astrophysicist who loved learning.

Perspective – Kieran Rose is an autistic author, trainer and advocate who shares his perspective to enhance the lives of autistic individuals.

Bravery – Greta Thunberg is an environmental activist who has shown bravery in advocating for positive environmental action from world leaders.

Perseverance – Dara McAnulty is an author and environmentalist.

Dara remembers specialists telling his parents that his life would be very limited. He persevered with his passion for nature writing to become a multi-award-winning author.

Honesty – Sir Anthony Hopkins is a very famous actor who is very honest about struggles he faced in his long acting career.

Zest – Usain Bolt is an Olympian sprinter and medallist. He channels his zest into his running.

Love – Louise Gooding is an author who wrote a book about neuro-diversity so that her daughter could read about other neurodivergent people.

Kindness – Daryl Hannah is an environmentalist and an actor. She demonstrates great kindness with her relentless environmental activism. She is trying very hard to make the world a better place for us all.

Social intelligence – Joan McDonald uses her social intelligence skills to support autistic individuals through her support network called Autistic Paddies.

Teamwork – Adam Harris is the CEO of a large autism charity in Ireland called As I Am. Adam Harris uses his character strength of teamwork every day, leading his team and meeting with people who can improve the lives of autistic people.

Fairness – Simone Biles is an Olympic-medal-winning gymnast. Some people said it was not fair for her to be taking ADHD (attention deficit hyperactivity disorder) medication while competing, but Simone argued that this was in fact fair.

Leadership – Yenn Purkis is an author that has held many leadership roles in their work as an autism advocate.

Forgiveness – Paige Layle is a well-known TikToker who demonstrates forgiveness by using her personal experience of being misdiagnosed before discovering she was autistic. Her TikTok content helps many people who are exploring their autistic identity.

Humility – The singer, Susan Boyle, always strikes me as a humble person, and this may be in part why her talent remained hidden for so long.

Prudence – Medallist and swimmer, Jessica-Jane Applegate, needs to use prudence to plan her intense training schedule.

Self-regulation – The actor, Emma Watson, requires strong self-regulation skills to maintain her demanding acting, modelling and United Nations career.

Appreciation of beauty and excellence – Aoife Dooley is an artist and illustrator who has appreciation of beauty and excellence as a character strength.

Gratitude – Billie Eilish is a very successful neurodivergent music artist. She was, of course, very grateful to her fans when she won four Grammys for her musical achievements.

Hope – Sean O'Mahony is a baker, known as the autistic baker, who offers hope to young autistic people wondering what they will do when they are older.

Humour – Hannah Gadsby is an autistic comedian. Much of her humour is geared towards an adult audience. She is, nevertheless, a strong autistic role model.

Spirituality – Olga Bogdashina is a well-known autism researcher and writer. She has researched autism and its links to spirituality.

Picture Books

Sharing picture books with your child can be such a bonding experience for you both. Exploring character strengths through picture books is both enjoyable and effective. Indeed, neuroscientists suggest that interaction and discussion during or following read-alouds stimulate high levels of brain activity (Roche 2020). *True You* by Kirsten Walton is a picture book that goes through a child-friendly explanation of each character strength. It is an ideal starting point for using picture books to explore strengths further. Following this, sharing well-loved books with your child is a great way to explore character strengths. Fairy tales, fables and classic children's tales often have a moral element that is ideal for exploring different strengths. For example, *The Little Mermaid* is one of my daughter's favourite tales. Through this tale it was possible to explore love, humility and appreciation of beauty and excellence. With older children and adolescents, it is possible to explore character strengths using the characters in novels. I have included some examples of character strengths embodied by characters in the *Harry Potter* series of novels. If your child likes cartoons, movies and television, use this interest to explore character strengths further. The following section includes recommendations of picture books that will help you and your child explore character strengths.

Ways to Generate Discussions about Strengths while Using Picture Books

The discussion you have with your child will depend on many factors, including age and stage of development, concentration and attention span, and level of interest in the book. Remember, it is very helpful for your child to generate questions too when discussing the book. *What, where, who* and *when* are generally easier to answer than *how* and *why*.

BEFORE READING

- Looking at the cover, what do you think this book will be about?
- Looking at the character on the cover, can you tell me anything about this person or their personality? Why do you think this?
- What strengths do you think this character might have? Why do you think this?

DURING READING

- Now that we have read this far, what can you tell me about the personality of...?
- What are their strengths?
- What in the book is telling you this?
- Does the villain show any character strengths?
- What character strengths would have helped them in this situation?
- Does the character remind you of anyone? In what way?
- Does the character remind you of yourself? In what way?

AFTER READING

- Did you enjoy the book?
- What did you enjoy about the book?
- Could the book have had a different ending?
- List all the character strengths in this book.
- Have you learned anything by reading this book?

Creativity

- *The Day the Crayons Quit*, **by Drew Daywalt and illustrated by Oliver Jeffers.** In this book, Duncan's crayons go on strike because they do not like how they are being used. Duncan tries creative ways to solve this problem.
- *Hum and Swish*, **by Matt Myers.** Jamie is a young girl who loves building in the sand close to the sea. One day she meets another artist at the seaside who also loves being creative.
- *Imagination Vacation*, **by Jami Gigot.** Sam's family is very busy and will never decide on the perfect holiday. Sam uses her character strength of creativity to plan a dream holiday for her hectic family to enjoy.
- *Not a Stick*, **by Antoinette Portis.** By using the character strength of creativity, a stick can become much more than a stick. It could become a magic wand, a conductor's baton and much, much more.
- *The Book of Mistakes*, **by Corinna Luyke.** This book explores how the creative process can often be a series of mistakes. The message of the book encourages a growth mindset.

Curiosity

- *Curiosity: The Story of a Mars Rover*, **by Markus Motum.** This picture book is about Curiosity, the robot that is currently exploring Planet Mars and sending back information to satisfy our curiosity here on Earth.
- *Windows*, **by Julia Denos.** A young boy takes his dog for a walk, and we experience what is going on behind the windows of the houses that he passes on his walk.
- *Papa's Mechanical Fish*, **by Candace Fleming.** This is the tale of a curious family whose father invents a wonderful submarine for his family.
- *On a Beam of Light*, **by Jennifer Berne.** This book is about Albert Einstein. It explores one of his signature character strengths, curiosity.

- *The Way Things Work*, **by David McCauley.** This non-fiction book will appeal to curious older readers.

Judgement

- *Big Al*, **by Andrew Clements and Yoshi.** This book teaches us not to judge sea animals by their appearance.
- *We're All Wonders*, **by R J Palacio.** My children love this picture book based on Auggie, a character from the novel *Wonder*. It encourages us to be non-judgemental about the differences we encounter in other people and ourselves.
- *The Hungry Coat – A Tale from Turkey*, **retold and illustrated by Demi.** This ancient tale from Turkey encourages the reader not to judge a person by what they wear.
- *Solomon the Wise King*, **by Simi Lu.** Solomon uses his signature character strength of judgement to solve a dispute between two women.
- *Demo: The Story of a Junkyard Dog*, **by Jon Bozak and illustrated by Scott Bruns.** In this book, we learn not to be misled by appearances and to be more discerning about what we discount and discard.

Love of Learning

- *Me...Jane*, **by Patrick McDonnell.** This book is a biography of Jane Goodall whose love of learning about living things led to an unusual and exciting life in Africa.
- *Abe Lincoln: The Boy Who Loved Books*, **by Kay Winters and illustrated by Nancy Carpenter.** This book describes a young Abraham Lincoln's love of learning, despite Lincoln having no formal education.
- *More than Anything Else*, **by Marie Bradby and illustrated by Chris K. Soentpiet.** This is a tale of a disadvantaged boy called Booker T. Washington. Booker's family need him to work as a manual labourer and Booker escapes his difficult life by reading books.
- *Mr. George Baker*, **by Amy Hest and illustrated by Jon J. Muth.**

George is a very elderly man who enlists the help of his neighbour, a young boy called Harry, in learning a skill.

- *Thank You Mr Falker*, **by Patricia Polacco.** In this story, a young girl named Trisha learns to taste the 'sweetness of knowledge' that her grandfather describes.

Perspective

- *Tales of Wisdom and Wonder*, **by Hugh Lupton and illustrated by Niamh Sharkey.** This is a collection of tales from around the world that explore the character strength of perspective.
- *The Pot of Wisdom: Anansi Stories*, **by Adwoa Badoe and illustrated by Baba Wagué Diakité.** This is another collection of tales that explore perspective. They feature Anansi the Spider and are based on popular African tales.
- *The Wise Woman and Her Secret*, **by Eve Merriam and illustrated by Linda Graves.** A young girl, through her sense of wonder, uncovers the secret to a wise woman's wisdom.
- *The Wisdom Bird: A Tale of Solomon and Sheba*, **by Sheldon Oberman and illustrated by Neil Waldman.** The Queen of Sheba visits the wise King Solomon with the hope of gaining his perspective. They both receive wisdom and perspective from a hoopoe bird.
- *Zomo the Rabbit: A Trickster Tale from West Africa*, **by Gerald McDermott.** In this tale, a rabbit asks the Sky God for wisdom. The rabbit is given a series of tasks to complete in order to receive wisdom.

Bravery

- *Tomorrow I'll Be Brave*, **written and illustrated by Jessica Hische.** This colourfully illustrated book encourages and motivates children to be brave.
- *Bold and Brave*, **by Kirsten Gillibrand and illustrated by Maira Kalman.** This book tells the story of ten brave American suffragettes.
- *Back of the Bus*, **by Aaron Reynolds and illustrated by Floyd**

Cooper. Rosa Park's story of bravery is retold from a child's perspective.

- *When Lions Roar,* **by Robbie H. Harris.** A young boy learns to bravely self-soothe when he is frightened of sounds in his environment.
- *The Little Yellow Leaf,* **written and illustrated by Carin Berger.** The little yellow leaf needs the help of his friends to become brave enough to leave his tree.

Perseverance

- *Amazing Grace,* **by Mary Hoffman.** This book is always well received when I read it in school. It is about a girl named Grace who pursues her goals with determination and perseverance.
- *Stuck,* **written and illustrated by Oliver Jeffers.** My children love this book. A young boy demonstrates great perseverance when his kite gets stuck in a tree.
- *The Name Jar,* **by Yangsook Choi.** This tale is another favourite, both at home and in school. A young Korean girl perseveres for her name to be pronounced correctly by her new classmates.
- *The Most Magnificent Thing,* **by Ashley Spires.** A little girl perseveres when her attempts at building an invention do not go to plan.
- *The Branch,* **by Mireille Messier.** Two neighbours make an unlikely pairing to persevere to create something out of a branch.

Honesty

- *The Boy Who Cried Wolf,* **retold by B. G. Hennessy.** This is a retelling of one of Aesop's best-loved fables. There are many illustrated retellings of the fable but this one is humorous and will appeal to readers of all ages.
- *The Honest-to-Goodness Truth,* **by Patricia McKissack and illustrated by Giselle Potter.** This book is a good way to explore the concept of curbing honesty for social reasons.

Libby's honesty at all times results in hurt feelings, and in this book, she learns that sometimes the truth helps and sometimes it hurts.

- *The Empty Pot*, **by Demi.** This continues to be one of my favourite picture books. This Chinese tale explores the honesty of a young boy hoping to be emperor.
- *Ruthie and the (Not So) Teeny Tiny Lie*, **by Laura Rankin.** In this tale, Ruthie lies to keep a camera she found that in fact does not belong to her.
- *Harriet and the Garden*, **by Nancy Carlson.** Harriet is a young bear who destroys a very special flower bed when playing with her ball. In this story, we learn not to hide from a situation just to avoid telling the truth.

Zest

- *Westlandia*, **by Paul Fleischman and illustrated by Kevin Hawkes.** This book describes the zest a boy called Wesley brings to his summer activities in his back garden.
- *Giraffe's Can't Dance*, **by Giles Andreae and Guy Parker-Rees.** Gerald the Giraffe demonstrates great grit and zest while learning to dance in his jungle home.
- *The Very Hungry Caterpillar*, **by Eric Carle.** This caterpillar munches his way through the week with zest.
- *Marco Polo*, **by Demi.** This is an exciting telling of the zestful adventures and explorations of Marco Polo.
- *I Am a Promise*, **by Shelly-Ann Fraser-Pryce, Ashley Rosseau and Rachel Moss.** This book tells the story of Shelly-Ann Fraser-Pryce, a zestful and inspiring Olympian.

Love

- *The Hug*, **by Eoin McLaughlin.** Hedgehog and tortoise both want a hug, but one has a hard shell and the other prickles. How will they find someone who will give them a hug?
- *I Love You, Stick Insect*, **by Chris Naylor-Ballesteros.** This is

a funny tale about a stick insect who falls deeply in love with a stick.

- *Mama, Do You Love Me?*, **by Barbara M. Joosse and illustrated by Barbara Lavallee.** This is a beautiful tale set in the arctic that is about unconditional parental love.
- *Love*, **by Matt de la Peña and illustrated by Loren Long.** This book explores many kinds of love.
- *Guess How Much I Love You*, **by Sam McBratney and illustrated by Anita Jeram.** This is a well-loved tale that explores the love between a parent and their child.

Kindness

- *Here We Are*, **by Oliver Jeffers.** This book helps the reader understand how to be kind to others.
- *My Heart*, **by Corinna Luyken.** In this book, the reader explores how to be kind to oneself as well as others.
- *Be Kind*, **by Pat Zietlow Miller and illustrated by Jen Hill.** The protagonist of this book is a young girl who tries to follow her mum's advice of 'be kind'.
- *A Boy Like You*, **by Frank Murphy.** This book shuns outdated stereotypes of boys and masculinity and shows that boys can be kind.
- *Pass it On*, **by Sophy Henn.** In this book, we are shown how simple acts of kindness can grow and have impact.

Social Intelligence

- *The Black Dog*, **by Levi Pinfold.** This is an amazing book that explores depression, incapacity and resilience.
- *My Heart Is a Compass*, **by Deborah Marcero.** This book shows us the wealth of creativity and imagination that lies within an individual.
- *In My Heart: A Book of Feelings*, **by Jo Witek.** This book can help your child explore emotions and how emotions feel in the body.
- *The Feelings Book*, **by Todd Parr.** This is a simple book and always a firm hit with my autistic pupils.

- *Town Is by the Sea*, **by Joanne Schwartz and Sydney Smith.** This is one of my favourite books and generates rich discussions about difficult emotions.

Teamwork

- *When Pencil Met Eraser*, **by Karen Kilpatrick and Luis O. Ramos Jr. and illustrated by Germán Blanco.** In this book, the two characters must work closely together but they have very different opinions. How will they sort this out?
- *The Curious Garden*, **by Peter Brown.** A young boy plants flowers that spread and enhance his local environment.
- *How the Ladies Stopped the Wind*, **by Bruce McMillan.** A group of ladies use teamwork to solve a problem in their home in Iceland.
- *Red and Yellow's Noisy Night*, **by Josh Selig.** Red and Yellow are friends that have very different sleeping patterns. They use collaboration and cooperation to solve this problem.
- *After the Rain*, **by Rebecca Koehn and illustrated by Simone Kruger.** Two friends use teamwork to decide what to do after the rain.

Fairness

- *Enemy Pie*, **by Derek Munson and illustrated by Tara Calahan King.** This book is always a favourite when I read it at home or in school. In this book, a dad is creative in teaching his son to give a new boy a fair chance.
- *Sidney, Stella and the Moon*, **by Emma Yarlett.** This is a firm favourite at bedtime in my house. It tells the tale of siblings who find it very difficult to share and be fair with each other and this difficulty leads to disastrous consequences!
- *It's Not Fair!*, **by Amy Krouse Rosenthal and illustrated by Tom Lichtenheld.** This book poses questions like, 'Why can't we get a pet giraffe?' and, in doing so, explores the character strength of fairness in an amusing way.
- *New Shoes*, **by Susan Lynn Meyer and illustrated by Eric**

Velásquez. This picture book brings the concept of fairness into the wider arena of social justice and explores racism and injustice in the civil rights era in America.

- *One Big Pair of Underwear,* **by Laura Gehl and illustrated by Tom Lichtenheld.** Here, fairness is explored through animals finding it difficult to share. It is both zany and funny.

Leadership

- *The Lost Thing,* **by Shaun Tan.** A boy shows great leadership skills when he finds a strange lost creature and strives to find out where it belongs.
- *Swimmy,* **by Leo Lionni.** Swimmy is a brave little fish who leads a school of fish who are hiding from danger.
- *Tacky the Penguin,* **by Helen Lester and illustrated by Lynn Munsinger.** This book teaches us that there is more than one type of leader and being different can bring great qualities to leadership.
- *Martin's Big Words: The Life of Dr. Martin Luther King, Jr.,* **by Doreen Rappaport and illustrated by Bryan Collier.** This is a visually appealing biography of Martin Luther King Jr. that is always popular with children whenever I read it with them.
- *The Little Engine That Could,* **by Watty Pipe.** This is a classic tale of the little engine who showed great leadership qualities.

Forgiveness

- *Lilly's Purple Plastic Purse,* **by Kevin Henkes.** Lilly seeks revenge when her teacher confiscates her favourite bag. She soon learns that forgiveness is more important than revenge.
- *Are We Still Friends?,* **by Ruth Horowitz.** Two friends fall out and need to make up before the new school year.
- *Benjamin and the Silver Goblet,* **by Jacqueline Jules.** This book is based on the Bible story of Joseph and his jealous and unkind brothers.
- *Friends Through Sand and Stone,* **by A. M. Marcus.** Rabbit and Monkey are friends whose relationship is tested during one of their adventures.

- *The Bad Mood and the Stick*, **by Lemony Snicket and illustrated by Matt Forsythe.** In this book, we learn that bad moods do not last forever and that forgiveness is important.

Humility

- *The Emperor's New Clothes*, **by Hans Christian Andersen.** A vain and proud emperor learns the value of humility through a very embarrassing lesson!
- *Humble Pie*, **by Jennifer Donnelly and illustrated by Stephen Gammell.** Theo's grandmother teaches him a lesson about humility by baking him a humble pie.
- *The Tower: A Story of Humility*, **by Richard Paul Evans and illustrated by Jonathan Linton.** A man believes he must build the tallest tower to be the greatest person in the land. He meets a bird and a wise old woman who teach him humility.
- *Osa's Pride*, **by Ann Grifalconi.** Osa is a proud girl who learns about the value of humility from her grandmother.
- *The Little Red Lighthouse and the Great Gray Bridge*, **by Hildegarde H. Swift and illustrated by Lynd Ward.** The little lighthouse feels humble next to the great grey bridge, but in this tale, the lighthouse learns that she is still of immense value.

Prudence

- *A Place for Everything*, **by Sean Covey and Stacy Curtis.** My children love this set of picture books based on Covey's Seven Habits. In this book, Jumper, a sports-loving rabbit, cannot find anything in his messy room and learns that everything should have a place.
- *Too Many Toys*, **by David Shannon.** In this story, the protagonist, Spencer, learns that it is prudent to keep his toys tidy so that he can always find his favourite toy to play with.
- *Lost and Found*, **by Oliver Jeffers.** This is another favourite with my children. A boy finds a penguin and methodically plans to return him to his home.

- *Shh!, We Have a Plan*, **by Chris Haughton.** The characters in this tale try to be prudent but fail miserably!
- *Prudence Wants a Pet*, **by Cathleen Daly and illustrated by Stephen Michael King.** Prudence really wants a pet and plays the long game to achieve her goal.

Self-Regulation

- *Max and Me*, **by Ines Lawlor and illustrated by Blanca Molto.** Max is a boy who has a 'modulator' in his brain that helps him self-regulate. I found this book invaluable when explaining self-regulation to my children.
- *Take Five*, **by Niall Breslin and illustrated by Sheena Dempsey.** In this book, Freddie's Granny helps him regulate his emotions.
- *How Do Dinosaurs Say I'm Mad?*, **by Jane Yolen and illustrated by Mark Teague.** This book is a witty take on how to regulate big emotions like anger.
- *The Great Big Book of Feelings*, **by Mary Hoffman and illustrated by Ros Asquith.** This book was always in my box of resources when I visited schools as a Health and Wellbeing Advisor. It is a great resource to help explore emotions and develop your child's emotional literacy.
- *Decibella and Her 6-Inch Voice*, **by Julia Cook and illustrated by Anita DuFalla.** Isabella has a very loud voice, and in this book, her teacher helps her regulate the volume of her voice.

Appreciation of Beauty and Excellence

- *The World Made a Rainbow*, **by Michelle Robinson and illustrated by Emily Hamilton.** This book combines an appreciation of the beauty of the natural world with the beauty of human nature, as a portion of the profits from this book will go to charity.
- *On a Beam of Light*, **by Jennifer Berne.** This picture book is a biography of Einstein and evokes a sense of wonder and awe in the reader.

- *I Wonder*, **by Annaka Harris and illustrated by John Rowe.** This book captures the beauty of life and the Universe.
- *Cloud Dance*, **by Thomas Locker.** Locker creates a journey in this book that allows us to appreciate the beauty and wonder of clouds.
- *Earth and I*, **by Frank Asch.** This book is a celebration of the friendship a child has with the Earth.

Gratitude

- *The Beckoning Cat: Based on a Japanese Folktale*, **by Koko Nishizuka and Rosanne Litzinge.** A boy is kind to a stray cat and the cat shows her gratitude, which benefits the boy's family.
- *The Giving Tree*, **by Shel Silverstein.** This is a classic tale of gratitude, involving a tree and a boy who grows as the tale unfolds.
- *Gratitude Soup*, **by Olivia Rosewood.** The author wrote this book to explain gratitude to her children in a fun and creative way.
- *Apple Cake*, **by Dawn Casey and illustrated by Genevieve Godbout.** In this book, a young girl gives thanks to nature.
- *Thanks a Million*, **by Nikki Grimes and illustrated by Cozbi A. Cabrera.** This is a gratitude-themed poetry book.

Hope

- *Rain Before Rainbows*, **by Smriti Prasadam-Halls and illustrated by David Litchfield.** In this beautifully illustrated book, a girl and a fox are forced to leave their home but face their journey with hope.
- *What We'll Build*, **by Oliver Jeffers.** This book, written in the form of a letter from a father to his daughter, is filled with the hope and dreams the father has for himself and his daughter.
- *Lost and Found Cat: The True Story of Kunkush's Incredible Journey*, **by Doug Kuntz and Amy Shrodes and illustrated by Sue Cornelison.** This book is about a family who never lose hope that they will be reunited with their long-lost cat.

- *Imagine*, **by John Lennon and illustrated by Jean Jullien.** In this picture book Lennon's lyrics are set to colourful illustrations of a pigeon spreading the message of hope around the world.
- *Little Mole Finds Hope*, **by Glenys Nellist.** Little Mole's mother helps him find hope in the midst of Winter.

Humour

- *The Giant's Loo Roll*, **by Nicolas Allan.** This is a must-read for any adult or child who likes toilet humour!
- *It's All About Me-Ow*, **by Hudson Talbott.** A humorous book written from the point of view of a cat.
- *Interrupting Chicken*, **by David Ezra Stein.** This humorous book will appeal to fairy-tale lovers.
- *Rosie's Walk*, **by Pat Hutchins.** This is a children's-book classic that will appeal to anyone who likes slapstick humour.
- *There's a Pig Up My Nose*, **by John Dougherty and illustrated by Laura Hughes.** This is a ridiculously funny picture book.

Spirituality

- *Ladder to the Moon*, **by Maya Soetoro-Ng and illustrated by Yuyi Morales.** This book explores the possibility of there being something bigger than ourselves and filling our hearts with compassion for others.
- *Zen Shorts*, **by Jon J. Muth.** A panda uses Zen parables to teach three children important values that enhance their spirituality.
- *Forever or a Day*, **by Sarah Jacoby.** This book helps the reader think about time and what it means to different people.
- *Grandad's Prayers of the Earth*, **by Douglas Wood and illustrated by P. J. Lynch.** During a forest walk, a young boy and his grandad talk about prayer and its meaning.
- *Three Questions*, **by Jon J. Muth.** Nikoli is a young boy who asks three questions in his quest to be a good person.

In Summary

▶ This chapter covers the *Explore* component of the IDEAS Framework.

▶ It outlines how to use mind maps when exploring strengths.

▶ It lists role models for each character strength, and most of these role models are neurodivergent.

▶ Strategies are shared that help explore strengths through literature, movies and picture books.

CHAPTER SIX

Action

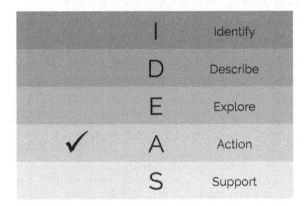

Introduction

So far, we have identified, described and explored your child's strengths, and now it is time to take further action, based on the knowledge and information you have gathered. In this chapter, Action, we will explore: why it is important to develop strengths; the optimal mindset to cultivate in both yourself and your child to promote strength development; how strengths can be underused, overused and misused; strengths optimization; strength regulation; and, of course, specific actions you and your child can take to develop strengths.

The identification and initial exploration of strengths is the beginning of an exciting journey of personal growth for your child. However, it is vital that your child is encouraged to take action and use and develop their strengths. It is interesting that in a study on strengths use, it was found that only seventeen percent of people use their strengths most of the time each day (Buckingham 2007). It is important to note that after simply labelling strengths, there can be a tendency for the individual not to take action, especially if strengths are viewed as fixed and defined. An example of this may be a child who has the character strength of creativity but does not work to develop the strength further by taking on, for instance, art activities that challenge and develop their creativity.

There are a few important factors to consider when taking action with strengths. It is vital to realize and to teach your child that character strengths are malleable. If it is possible, encourage your child to view strengths as personal traits to cultivate and as having the potential to aid flourishing (Biswas-Diener, Kashdan and Minhas 2011). It is worth noting that taking action to realize the full potential of your child's strengths takes time, commitment and effort. It involves focus on skills development and what Diener describes as 'deep work'.

This chapter aims to change the traditional tendency to overinvest time and energy into overcoming challenges that the autistic individual faces. Instead, the hope is that you will be encouraged to adopt what is called a growth mindset and harness the potential of your child's strengths to help them flourish and thrive.

Growth and Fixed Mindsets

Mindset is very important when it comes to believing that action can help your child fully realize their strengths. There are, broadly speaking, two types of mindsets that have an influence on how we take action with strengths: a fixed mindset and a growth mindset. Carol Dweck has researched mindsets and written widely on them (2006, 2012, 2015, 2016, 2017a, 2017b). If you find the concept of mindsets interesting, I recommend that you read Dweck's work, as Dweck herself states that there has been much misunderstanding and misinformation about mindsets that has led to some criticism of her work. Having a growth mindset is more than keeping an open mind, praising effort and telling children that they can do anything (Dweck 2017a). Therefore, before we take action, we will explore fixed and growth mindsets.

A fixed mindset is detrimental to strength development. A person with a fixed mindset is more likely to believe that great things will follow from merely possessing the strength, regardless of effort or action. With a fixed mindset, there may well be a tendency to blame lack of achievement on strengths or lack of strengths in a particular area. There is likely to be more emphasis on appearances, for example, a child could use their creativity and say, 'I drew this great picture,' rather than taking real action in using their strengths, for example, saying, 'I really like drawing animals, how can I become even better at drawing them?'

A person with a fixed mindset is likely to:

- believe that character strengths are fixed and cannot be developed over time
- believe that ability, talents and intelligence are static and cannot be noticeably changed
- avoid failure and mistakes
- want to be seen as skilled, clever and knowledgeable
- avoid risk-taking and challenges
- shy away from feedback.

In contrast, a growth mindset is very beneficial when taking action with strengths development. With a growth mindset, there is a belief and an attitude that strengths can be developed and improved. There is a willingness to put effort and work into personal growth. Setbacks and mistakes are seen as opportunities for learning rather than failures.

A person with a growth mindset is likely to:

- believe that character strengths are malleable and can and should be developed over time
- believe that talents and intelligence can be improved with effort
- see mistakes as learning opportunities
- like being described as a trier and determined
- see learning as a process that involves risk-taking and challenges
- welcome feedback and constructive criticism as a powerful way to learn.

There is great hope in knowing that mindsets can be changed. It is important for parents to model growth mindsets for their children. However, there are further actions that you can take to cultivate a growth mindset in your child:

- Praise effort rather than ability.
- If your child does not succeed at first with their efforts, review the activity by asking questions like: Was the activity pitched at the right level of challenge? What can be done to support success?
- Add 'yet' to your child's fixed mindset statements, for example, 'I can't ride a bike... yet,' and 'I can't draw a unicorn...yet.'
- If you think your child will respond well to this, try explaining neuroplasticity, that is, that our brain is amazing and is always changing and developing.
- Use the positive statements about strengths in Chapter Four, *Describe*, and consider writing them in your child's strengths diary.

There is research available on mindsets and autism that is helpful to share when we are considering taking action with character strengths. For example, Brooks and Goldstein (2013) wrote about the importance of developing a mindset, similar to a growth mindset, in autistic children and young people that helps the child feel like they have an element of control in their life, have problem-solving skills and know how to set goals. They call this a socially resilient mindset. Brooks and Goldstein advocate for adopting a strengths-based approach when supporting autistic children and young people.

Strength Regulation

It is also critically important to regulate the use and development of our strengths. To illustrate the importance of this, let us look at the following example. A relative calls at your house with a gift for your child. One of your child's signature strengths is honesty. If your child uses their strength in an unregulated way, they are likely to exclaim in horror if they dislike the gift. A child who has learned about their strength and how and when to regulate honesty is more likely to thank their relative for the gift.

When thinking about action in relation to strengths, it is helpful to consider how well your child can use their strengths to enhance their wellbeing. For example, if your child loves video games and one of their strengths is perseverance, they may well be tempted to ignore their basic needs to complete the levels of the game. However, if they possess another strength, like prudence, they may be able to regulate their use of perseverance to moderate their game play and take regular breaks to move, rest, eat and drink. How well your child will be able to call on the right strength for a given situation depends on several factors and is influenced by age and stage of development. Most children would need this sophisticated use of strengths modelled and scaffolded for them by an adult.

When taking action with strengths, it is important to prioritize strength development as well as strength use (Biswas-Diener *et al.* 2011). This involves looking at different contexts and goals and seeing how each strength can be best developed and used in these situations.

Strength Overuse, Underuse and Misuse

When exploring taking action with strengths, it is important to highlight that strengths can be misused and overused. Strengths misuse can cause harm to the individual and others. An example of strengths misuse might be someone using the character strength of humour to poke fun at someone and, by doing so, hurt their feelings. Overusing strengths can have a negative impact on your child's wellbeing. Examples of strengths overuse would be using zest to exercise to excess or bravery to engage in a risky behaviour.

So, in taking action with strengths, what you as a parent are aiming for is for your child to engage in optimal strength use and development. Here are a few suggestions that will optimize your child's character strengths. You know your child best and will know which activities are worth trying. Activities that do not work now may well work in the future. Your child will benefit from these strategies being modelled and supported, and this will give your child a good chance at success.

Taking Action to Cultivate Individual Strengths

In this section, suggestions are given for cultivating every character strength. I have also included descriptions of what underuse and overuse may look like or how a strength's underuse or overuse may be perceived by others. This information is adapted with permission from Niemiec (2017). It is important to recognize that children are busy developing and exploring their strengths as part of their creation of self-identity. Therefore, underusing and overusing their character strengths is to be expected and is indeed a healthy part of development. Nevertheless, I think as parents it is useful to have a strengths vocabulary that includes descriptions of strength underuse and overuse.

Creativity

Peterson and Seligman (2004) suggest that creativity is nurtured in homes that are supportive and open. Ideally, provide multiple opportunities for stimulating creativity, like having books, comics and art materials available for your child. It is important to develop your child's interests so that they can have the opportunity to develop expertise, which is linked to creativity. Creativity is one of the most frequently found strengths in children. Time limits, overly close supervision and critical inspection can limit its development. When creativity is underused, it is expressed as conformity. When it is overused, it is often described as eccentricity (Niemiec 2017).

- Be wary of time pressures and overly close supervision. Brainstorming ideas is an activity that is closely associated with creativity.
- Introducing the idea of putting ideas aside and returning to them is also helpful in the cultivation of creativity.
- Encourage different creative processes, such as junk art, construction, visual art, writing, digital media, baking, drama and music.
- Get involved with your child's creative projects by co-creating and providing constructive feedback and specific praise.
- When there is a product from your child's creativity, celebrate it.

Curiosity

This is one of five strengths linked with happiness. Curiosity is one of the most commonly identified strengths. It is connected with several protective factors, including longevity and positive relationships. Its underuse is associated with disinterest and its overuse is expressed as nosiness (Niemiec 2017).

- Provide new experiences. Curiosity is activated by the person interacting with their environment.
- Learning opportunities should have an appropriate amount of challenge – neither too easy nor too difficult.
- Having a mentor can ignite curiosity. For example, having a friend or significant adult who is also curious about a topic or experience.

Judgement

This is one of the five most commonly identified strengths in individuals who take the VIA Survey. It is a strength that protects against manipulation by others. When underused, it can present as an individual being unreflective. Its overuse can make the individual appear narrow-minded (Niemiec 2017).

- Model being open-minded.
- Encourage critical thinking.
- Discuss stories like fairy tales from the point of view of the villains.

Love of Learning

This strength is linked to wellbeing and self-efficacy. When love of learning is underused, it can appear that the individual is being complacent, and when it is overused, the individual may come across to others as a know-it-all (Niemiec 2017).

- Model a love of learning by engaging in learning yourself.
- Engage in positive talk about learning and the process of learning.
- Encourage the learning process and interests.
- Provide different modes of accessing information.
- Facilitate friendships based on shared interests.
- Praise and encourage effort when learning.
- Explore role models who demonstrate a love of learning.
- Discuss characters in books, movies and cartoons that display a love of learning.

Perspective

This strength is linked with positive ageing experiences and can help protect against the negative effects of trauma and stress. If this strength is underused, it can appear that the individual is being shallow, and when it is overused, an individual may seem overbearing (Niemiec 2017).

- Being mentored or mentoring is associated with the development of perspective (Smith, Staudinger and Baltes 1994).
- It is important for children to have opportunities to engage in varied opportunities for learning.
- Read classic tales like Aesop's fables and discuss their meaning.

Bravery

Bravery has the potential to lower anxiety and helps build resilience. Its underuse can be expressed as cowardice and its overuse is seen in foolhardy and risky behaviours (Niemiec 2017).

- Explore situations that your child finds daunting and scary. Troubleshoot and problem solve. For example, try the hairdressers early in the morning so that there is less noise.
- Model bravery and share experiences and examples of when you have had to be brave in your life.
- Explore everyday examples of bravery. Bravery does not have to be about dragon and monster slaying.

Perseverance

When perseverance is underused, it looks like helplessness, and when it is overused, it has an obsessive quality (Niemiec 2017).

- Write, draw and describe goals.
- Break goals down into TATS – tiny achievable targets.
- Praise and reward effort and process over end results.
- Give specific feedback along the way to achieving a goal.

Honesty

Honesty is one of the five most common character strengths. If it is underused, an individual may come across as phony, and if it is overused, an individual can seem overly blunt and righteous (Niemiec 2017).

- Give specific praise when your child is honest. Naming the behaviour, that is, saying, 'You are being honest,' is effective in promoting honesty (Casey and Burton 1982).
- Higher levels of honesty are detected in children who experience higher levels of trust in their family environment (Abeler, Falk and Kosse 2021).
- When your child does wrong, the anticipated consequence for their wrongdoing influences how honest they will be. Make it explicit to your child that honesty is valued in these situations.
- It may help your child to explore times when curbing their honesty is socially appropriate. Statements about people's physical appearance and voicing dislike of a gift are two examples where not voicing honesty may be appropriate.

Zest

This is one of the strengths most commonly linked to life satisfaction and one of the least commonly identified character strengths. It is, perhaps unsurprisingly, linked to positive health outcomes. An individual who is underusing zest may appear to be sedentary in their behaviours and its overuse may be expressed in hyperactivity (Niemiec 2017).

- Give your child plenty of opportunities to use their zest by providing active and outdoor play experiences.
- Allow your child to cultivate their interests and passions.
- If your child likes surprises, bring a sense of wonder and surprise to everyday activities.
- Maintain zest by trying as much as possible to keep to a regular sleep schedule.

Love

Love is also strongly linked to life satisfaction and is very often identified as a character strength in young children. Love is associated with strong and positive relationships. Its underuse is expressed as emotional isolation and its overuse as an emotional promiscuity (Niemiec 2017).

- Explore different types of love with your child. Linking love to relationship circles is a helpful way to explore different types of relationships with your child.
- Where possible, model healthy and loving relationships for your child.
- Be open to discussions about romantic love with your child.

Kindness

Kindness is one of the five most common character strengths found in individuals. Possessing the character strength of kindness helps protect against the negative effects of trauma and stress. An individual who underuses this strength may seem indifferent to others, and when kindness is overused, it can seem intrusive (Niemiec 2017).

- Model acts of kindness and speak kindly about others in the presence of others.
- Value acts of kindness and give your child specific praise when they are kind to others.
- Practise being kind to yourself and let your child see you doing this.
- Read books about kindness and point out to your child when a character in a book or movie is being kind.
- Have a random acts of kindness (RAK) challenge in your family.

Social Intelligence

Social intelligence also helps protect against the harmful effects of trauma and stress. A person who underuses their social intelligence may appear insensitive, and an individual who overuses this strength may seem to be overanalyzing social interactions (Niemiec 2017).

- Practise naming emotions and emotion coaching with your child. If you see that your child is happy, name the emotion and tell your child explicitly why you think they are happy (smiling, stimming, clapping hands).

- Explain your emotions to your child. If you use strategies to manage your emotions, make these explicit to your child (deep breathing, naming and taming, counting to ten).
- Explore emotions using books, music, art, cartoons and movies.
- Do not label emotions in negative terms. All emotions are valid, even if some are uncomfortable.
- Make your child safe in the knowledge that all emotions are valid.

Teamwork

Individuals who consistently underuse this strength are sometimes seen as selfish in their behaviours, and when teamwork is overused by an individual, it could be interpreted as being overly dependent on others (Niemiec 2017).

- Play games that involve teamwork, collaboration and cooperation. These could be active games like relays or simple ball games, or games like charades and Pictionary.
- Co-create cleaning rosters for the home. Allow your child to choose something that they are good at and can do with some degree of independence.
- Vote on what to have for dinner or what movie to watch at the weekend.
- Use memberships to clubs, leisure centres and afterschool activities as an opportunity to explore teamwork and social responsibility.

Fairness

Fairness is one of the most commonly identified strengths. If it is underused, there is the possibility that the individual can seem detached, and if it is overused, the individual may seem to be engaging in partisan behaviours (Niemiec 2017).

- Parenting is a very important factor in developing a child's sense of fairness. Democratic family decision-making can help develop the character strength of fairness (Peterson and Seligman 2004).

- Create role plays, maybe involving puppets that act out scenarios to explore whether a situation is fair or not.
- Involve your child in decision-making and make the decision-making process explicit to them.
- Provide plentiful and varied social experiences.
- Model being open-minded and being appreciative of difference (Peterson and Seligman 2004).

Leadership

A person who underuses this strength can be overly compliant, and if leadership is overused, it can come across as bossiness or even despotism (Niemiec 2017).

- Give opportunities to your child to cultivate leadership by carefully scaffolding leadership roles. For example, if you are planning a surprise party, have a designated role for everyone in the family and allow your child to choose who will carry out each role.
- Model strong advocacy for your child.
- Give your child responsibility in the house at a level that provides a little challenge. This could be something as simple as watering the plants.

Forgiveness

Possessing forgiveness as a character strength is associated with many positive wellbeing benefits like fewer feelings of anger, anxiety and depression. An individual who underuses forgiveness may be perceived as lacking mercy. If it is overused, an individual may seem overly permissive (Niemiec 2017).

- Use the 4F framework outlined in Chapter Four, *Describe*.
- Model forgiveness for your child and be forgiving towards your child.
- Read stories where the benefits of forgiveness are explored.
- Explain the possible intent behind the behaviour that caused harm; oftentimes, there is no malicious intent, and many incidents are accidental.

- Remember that forgiveness is a character trait that develops with age.

Humility

Humility is one of the least commonly identified strengths. It is associated with strong social connections. If it is underused, an individual can appear as arrogant, and if it is overused, humility can be seen as self-deprecating behaviour (Niemiec 2017).

- Helping your child feel secure and safe helps nurture humility.
- Teach your child that constructive feedback and criticism is something worth listening to.
- Accurate and evidence-based praise helps maintain humility.

Prudence

Prudence is also not a very commonly endorsed strength. It is strongly associated with health and wellbeing. If it is underused, an individual can be perceived as being thrill-seeking, and if it is overused, an individual can seem stuffy in their behaviour (Niemiec 2017).

- Help your child make plans. One approach that works very well comes from the CO-OP approach that is often used by occupational therapists. A core feature of the CO-OP approach is a four-step guide to planning.
  1. *Goal* – What is it that you want to achieve?
  2. *Plan* – How are you going to achieve your goal?
  3. *Do* – Carry out the plan.
  4. *Check* – Evaluate, how well did the plan work?[1]

Self-Regulation

Parents can teach their children to self-regulate through co-regulation, which involves modelling self-regulation strategies. It also helps a child's self-regulation if the parent provides routine, structure and predictability, and manages transitions and change effectively by explicitly praising

---

[1] This bullet point was inspired by Polatajko, H. and Mandich, A. (2004) 'Enabling Occupation in Children: The CO-OP Approach.' Nepean, ON: Canadian Association of Occupational Therapists. CAOT publications, ACE.

efforts to self-regulate and providing a safe, secure and low-arousal environment (Perry and Hambrick 2008). Other strategies that help develop and support self-regulation include the following:

- Adapt the sensory and physical environment to suit your child. A tent or a calm corner is a great self-regulation tool.
- Use sensory supports to aid regulation. The Alert Program™ and The Zones of Regulation are two interventions that I have used with success.
- Teach your child about their emotions. This includes naming their emotions as they are experiencing them. The Zones of Regulation, when adapted to suit the individual, and Emotion Coaching are two approaches that I find helpful.
- Let your child know that all emotions are okay but sometimes the action that goes with the emotion is not okay.
- Breath work is very effective.
- In my experience, yoga (especially chanting and breathing) and rhythmical and repetitive exercise like walking are very regulating for autistic children.
- A self-regulation toolkit and/or basket with a number of regulating aids is very helpful.

Appreciation of Beauty and Excellence

This strength is associated with healthy behaviours. A person who underuses this strength may appear oblivious to the beauty in the world and the individual who overuses this strength may appear to be perfectionistic (Niemiec 2017).

- Model this character strength for your child. Explicitly tell them about what you appreciate in terms of awe and wonder in the natural, cultural and social world you and your child inhabit.
- Create opportunities for your child to see beauty all around them. Nature walks are great for this. If your child is interested, bring a magnifying glass and other nature exploration aids like pooters. Visit different natural settings like lakes,

forests, beaches, unusual landscapes, gardens and wildlife centres.

- If your child shows an interest, explore the wonders of the Universe through visits to planetariums and observatories, telescopes, books, documentaries and shorter video clips on the internet.
- Your child may experience appreciation of beauty and excellence in music, art or architecture. Give them as many opportunities as you can to experience this.
- If your child keeps a journal, they could add their awe and wonder moments to their journal. This, of course, could be a regular entry in their strengths diary.

Gratitude

Gratitude is very strongly associated with life satisfaction and wellbeing. When it is underused, it presents as entitlement, and when it is overused, it presents as ingratiating or fawning behaviour (Niemiec 2017). Fawning is a behaviour very commonly associated with autistic individuals, so it is worth carefully supporting the development of this character strength (Pearson, Rees and Rose 2022). A gratitude practice is something that grows easier with time and perseverance. In my experience, it is a practice well worth pursuing. I have used the suggestions below with very positive outcomes with autistic children.

- At mealtime, have each person say one thing that they are grateful for that day. You may have to model this for a while before your child will join in.
- At bedtime, list three things that you are grateful for and ask your child to do the same.
- If your child finds this difficult, name some things that your child did or said during the day that made you grateful.
- Your child may find it easier to write or draw what it is that they are grateful for. It is great to have a special journal or a section of their strengths diary for this.
- Alternatively, have a bank of visuals that your child can choose from.

Hope

This is a strength strongly associated with life satisfaction. If hope is underused, the individual's behaviour can appear pessimistic. Its overuse can present as Pollyannaism, named after a fictional character, Pollyanna, who saw the positive side in even the direst situations (Niemiec 2017).

- Model hopeful statements like: 'If I save for the next two weeks, we can all go to the cinema and go for pizza afterwards.'
- Make plans with your children and make the planning process achievable. For example, if they want to buy a new video game, break down the steps they will need to undertake to earn it.
- Planning tools like to-do lists and daily schedules help cultivate hope.
- Reward children – not only when a plan is achieved but also for reaching steps along the way.
- Be your child's coach when they are stuck on a problem instead of providing the solution. Ask questions like, 'What else can you try?' and 'What do you already know that will help you with this?'
- Using role models as examples is especially helpful when cultivating hope.
- Reading books with hopeful themes helps generate hope (McDermott and Hastings 2000).

Humour

Humour is very strongly associated with life satisfaction and positive emotions. It is also linked to health and wellbeing. If humour is underused, someone can appear to be overly serious, and if it is overused, an individual's behaviour can be described as giddy and silly (Niemiec 2017).

- Keep a humour (joke, pun, riddle) diary with your child or have a humour section in your child's strengths diary.
- Draw humorous pictures and cartoons.
- Take turns to tell jokes on a chosen day during the week or at the dinner table.
- Watch comedy and funny movies together.

- Read humorous books with your child.
- Take joke books out from the library.
- Tell an incomplete joke and have your child finish it.
- Use a humorous calendar in the home.
- Encourage play and playfulness.
- Teach your child explicitly that humour should make others feel good and should not be a tool to hurt or belittle others.

Spirituality

Spirituality is associated with positive relationships. When overused, the associated behaviour is often described as fanaticism (Niemiec 2017).

- Reflect on your own spiritual beliefs and understanding. This will help you support your child's developing spirituality.
- If you follow a religious faith, involve your child in your religious community.
- Meet your child where they are at in their understanding of spirituality. Answer their questions as best you can.
- If you are religious, celebrate the spiritual element of religious holidays. Symbolism, art and icons will help with this.
- Read child-friendly versions of religious texts to your child and discuss their meaning.
- Introduce your child to prayer and/or meditation.
- Encourage a sense of wonder and awe in the natural world and the Universe.
- Find examples to emphasize the interconnectedness of human beings.

Taking Action Activities

I have named the following exercises Taking Action Activities. For all these activities I would recommend using your child's strengths diary or a scrapbook. Please record your child's activities in varied ways such as written entries, pictures, photographs and completed worksheets. Most of these activities have been adapted with permission from Ryan Niemiec's work on character strengths interventions (2017).

Strengths Self-Reflection and Monitoring

What Is This Taking Action Activity?

It can be very helpful to have an evening practice where you reflect with your child on their strengths use during the day. This practice will need to be adapted to suit your child. With younger children, asking a few questions at dinnertime or at bedtime may be sufficient. It also might suit your child better to focus on one strength for a period before moving on to another. For older children who have developed the ability to be reflective, a written exercise like the worksheet at the end of this chapter can be very effective. This can be done in their strengths diary.

How to Do This Taking Action Activity

1. Take a target strength and reflect on this strength at the end of each day.
   - Did you use your strength today?
   - Can you give me an example of when you used your strength today?

   More challenging questions for a child that is familiar with this exercise.
   - Did you overuse any of your strengths today?
   - Did you misuse any of your strengths today?
   - Were there any situations where you could have used a strength but did not think of it?
2. Record answers and observations in your child's strengths diary.

Why Use This Taking Action Activity?

This activity helps children think about their strengths and makes them more aware of how they can use their strengths in different situations.

If Your Child Finds This Taking Action Activity Challenging

For younger children and children who find this activity difficult, please review the day with them by asking about a particular strength. With this activity, it is important to create a safe atmosphere where your child knows that this is a reflective exercise to improve their strengths use. It would be very helpful for you to model the use of the questions, and it may be beneficial to do this for a period of time before your child attempts to reflect on their strengths. Hearing you reflect on strength overuse, underuse and misuse will help your child realize that everyone must practise using their strengths and that making mistakes and adjusting strength use is a positive trait to be cultivated.

Use a Strength in a New Way[2]

What is This Taking Action Activity?

This is a classic PPI that has been used and researched widely (Gander *et al.* 2013, Seligman *et al.* 2005). It is, in fact, one of the most cited PPIs in positive psychology (Niemiec 2017).

How to Do This Taking Action Activity

1. Have your child's list of signature strengths to hand.
2. Select one of your child's signature strengths.
3. Plan ways to use this strength in new ways for a week. Give an appropriate amount of support with this.
4. Carry out the plan and record the activity in your child's strengths diary or on the worksheet provided.
5. Debrief this activity with your child and consider repeating the activity with a new strength from your child's list.

Why Use This Taking Action Activity?

It enhances your child's awareness of their strengths by using their best traits.

If Your Child Finds This Taking Action Activity Challenging

*   Reread the 'Signature Strengths' section in Chapter Two, *The Foundations*.
*   Look at the 'Taking Action to Cultivate Individual Strengths' section of this chapter.
*   Examine how people with similar strengths to your child use

---

2   Adapted with permission from Niemiec 2017, CSI 11.

their strength. This could be a role model, historical figure, fictional character, friend or family member.

- Do not forget the value of modelling this exercise and talking about the process explicitly.

Adaptation – Using Strengths in Different Life Domains

Ask your child to think about an area of their life that might need some change. For an older child, this could be something like homework and study. Ask your child to think of a strength that they possess that might help them with that life domain. For example, if your child is creative, it might be that they design a new study timetable with your help.

Acting 'As If'[3]

What Is This Taking Action Activity?

This PPI was first created by Alfred Adler (1963). This is one of the first PPIs that I experienced and benefitted from. There is a powerful lesson in acting 'as if' and not waiting for the right time to try something.

How to Do This Taking Action Activity

1. Select a strength. It is a good idea to choose a strength that others see in your child but that your child may not be too confident in using. Your child could also choose a strength that they would like to develop.
2. Choose a specific situation where you would like to use the strength. For example, it could be using bravery or zest to use a piece of playground equipment that seems daunting. Try to use a situation or a task that is just slightly out of your child's comfort zone so there is more likely to be success.
3. Help your child visualize using the strength in the situation. Draw on the senses to really shape this visualization.
4. Try using the qualities of the character strength to complete the activity.
5. Debrief this activity with your child. Praise the effort involved.
6. Record in your child's strengths diary.

---

3   Adapted with permission from Niemiec 2017, CSI 12.

Why Use This Taking Action Activity?

This activity may help your child boost the use of a strength that is underused. It may also be used to develop a strength that your child wants to cultivate.

If Your Child Finds This Taking Action Activity Challenging

This can be a challenging Taking Action Activity. If the exercise has been unsuccessful, it is even more important to praise the effort taken. Review the exercise and see if the plan can be broken down into TATs. For example, if the plan were to use zest and bravery in order to use a new piece of playground equipment, maybe use the equipment with adult support. Alternatively, help your child visualize several 'as if' scenarios and plan them in TATs. The action piece can happen at a later stage (Watts 2013).

Using a Strength for Oneself[4]

What Is This Taking Action Activity?

I love this Taking Action Activity, as it is very much related to a powerful branch of mindfulness called mindfulness-based self-compassion. This activity takes character strengths that are usually related to being directed towards others (e.g. love, kindness, forgiveness and fairness) and turns them inwards to nurture the individual. This activity is more suited to older children and teenagers.

How to Do This Taking Action Activity

1. Ask your child to think of a time where they were not at their best. Maybe they were unkind or made a mistake.
2. Use a rating scale of one to ten to help your child rate the following.
   - How kind were you to yourself after this event?
   - How forgiving were you to yourself after this event?
   - How well did you use perspective after this event happened?

---

4   Adapted with permission from Niemiec 2017, CSI 13.

You can, of course, ask a variation of these questions using different strengths.

3. Ask your child how they use these character strengths with others and how they can now use them to benefit themselves.
4. Record responses in your child's strengths diary.

Why Use This Taking Action Activity?

Self-compassion is a powerful skill that can be cultivated by turning character strengths like love and kindness inward.

If Your Child Finds This Taking Action Activity Challenging

This is a challenging Taking Action Activity. If your child finds it too challenging at the minute, consider using mindfulness-based intentions that come from mindfulness-based self-compassion. Examples of these include:

- May I be kind.
- May I be loved.
- May I be safe.
- May I be calm.

These intentions are usually said with one's dominant hand resting on one's chest, which is an action of self-compassion.

Making a Habit of a Strength[5]

What Is This Taking Action Activity?

This Taking Action Activity helps your child enhance their signature strengths and lesser strengths by taking small but effective actions.

How to Do This Taking Action Activity

1. Choose a character strength with your child that they would like to develop. To begin with, it may be easier to pick a

---

5 Adapted with permission from Niemiec 2017, CSI 14.

signature strength, but with practice, your child could work on a lesser strength.

2. Choose a **cue**. For example, this could be every time your child sits down to dinner.
3. Start a new **routine**. For example, this could be using gratitude to thank whoever made the meal and saying one thing that is nice about the meal.
4. **Reward** your child's use of the character strength by telling them one thing you are grateful for in terms of their behaviour.

Why Use This Taking Action Activity?
This Taking Action Activity helps model healthy habit-making behaviours.

If Your Child Finds This Taking Action Activity Challenging
If your child finds this challenging, try linking the habit-forming loop of cue, routine and reward to activities or situations of high interest to your child.

Develop a Lower Strength[6]
What Is This Taking Action Activity?
There are often very valid reasons for developing lower strengths. For example, self-regulation is one of the least common signature strengths and not only amongst autistic individuals. It is, however, a character strength I work hard to support in myself, my children and the autistic children and adults that I support in my teaching and coaching. Lower strengths are also known as lesser strengths.

How to Do This Taking Action Activity

1. Choose one of your child's lower strengths. Ideally have a sound rationale for choosing this lesser strength.
2. Use the strength in a new way each day.
3. Provide the support your child will need to use the strength. For example, if you choose self-regulation, have a

---

6 Adapted with permission from Niemiec 2017, CSI 19.

self-regulation toolbox for your child and teach them how to use it.

4. Record progress in your child's strengths diary.

Why Use This Taking Action Activity?
To develop a lower strength that is potentially useful for your child.

If Your Child Finds This Taking Action Activity Challenging
Be very selective in the lower strengths that you choose. This involves choosing strengths that will add value to your child's life in some way.

STRENGTHS SELF-REFLECTION AND MONITORING SHEET ONE

Target strength: . . . .

Did I use my target strength today?

Yes   No

On a scale of 1 to 5, how well did I use this strength today?

1   2   3   4   5

Examples of when I used my target strength today:

1. . . . .

2. . . . .

3. . . . .

STRENGTHS SELF-REFLECTION AND MONITORING SHEET TWO

Target strength(s): . . . .

Did I use my target strength(s) today?

    Yes   No

On a scale of 1 to 5, how well did I use this strength/these strengths today?

    1   2   3   4   5

Examples of when I used my target strength(s) today:

    1. . . . .

    2. . . . .

    3. . . . .

Did I overuse any of my strengths today?

    Yes   No   Describe: . . . .
. . . .

Did I misuse any of my strengths today?

    Yes   No   Describe: . . . .
. . . .

Were there any situations where I could have used a strength but did not think of it?

    Yes   No   Describe: . . . .
. . . .

USE A STRENGTH IN A NEW WAY

My signature strengths

1. . . . .

2. . . . .

3. . . . .

4. . . . .

5. . . . .

This week I choose . . . . to use in a new way.

This is my plan for using . . . . in a new way:

Day	Plan
Sunday	. . . .
Monday	. . . .
Tuesday	. . . .
Wednesday	. . . .
Thursday	. . . .
Friday	. . . .
Saturday	. . . .

In Summary

▶ This chapter covers the *Action* component of the IDEAS Framework.
▶ Growth and fixed mindsets are explored.
▶ Strength regulation is discussed.
▶ Strength overuse, underuse and misuse are discussed.
▶ Each of the 24 VIA character strengths is taken in turn, and actionable tips and strategies are given for each strength.
▶ A number of Taking Action Activities are outlined.

CHAPTER SEVEN

Support

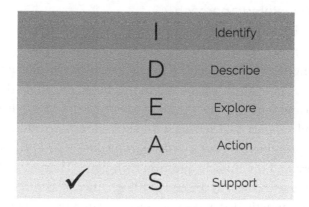

We have reached the final chapter of the IDEAS Framework. This chapter, Support, is written to help you to continue to use a strengths-based approach with your child both now and, hopefully, long into the future. In order for your child to fully realize the potential of their character strengths, it is essential that they are supported in a comprehensive way. Having engaged with the information and activities contained within the IDEAS Framework, you are in a strong position to figure out what should happen next for you and your child in terms of using a strengths-based approach. After much research into the topic of supporting strengths, I decided to use Rapp, Saleebey and Sullivan's 2006 framework, which is based around six standards that outline a way to continue to support your child in taking a strengths-based approach.

Standards of a Strengths-Based Approach

1. Goal-orientated approach
2. Assessment of strengths
3. Environment
4. Resources
5. Relationships
6. Choice

1. Goal-Orientated Approach

The first characteristic of this approach is that it should be in some way goal orientated. This means that you and your child will be using their strengths to achieve goals. There are many ways to set goals, some of which we have already explored in this book, including the CO-OP approach and setting TATs. I think it is worthwhile to explicitly teach, model and support goal setting with your child. Two additional goal-setting approaches that work well are using the SMARTER goal-setting framework and the miracle question technique. There is a SMARTER goal-setting worksheet at the end of this chapter. The miracle question technique is an activity that is sometimes used in support approaches like coaching, Solution-Focused Therapy (SFT) and Cognitive-Behavioural Therapy (CBT). The approach starts by asking your child a question like:

> I would like you to imagine that while you were sleeping, a miracle happened. While you slept, your goal magically came into being. When you got up out of bed, what did you notice?

After asking this initial question, a good approach would be to flesh out the answer in your child's strengths diary. Help your child to visualize the achieved goal in as much detail as possible. Additional questions can really contribute to the goal-setting process. Here are some examples:

- What is your energy level?
- What emotions are you feeling?
- What did you do to achieve your goal?
- What is different after achieving your goal?

2. Assessment of Strengths

We explored how to assess your child's strengths in Chapter Three, *Identify*. Your child's strengths diary is a continuous assessment of their strengths. Furthermore, in school, your child is likely to have new members of school staff working with them on at least an annual basis. It would be helpful to check in with them and see if they notice things like new, previously undiscovered strengths in your child. They may also notice how a strength is developing and new ways to use a particular strength. It is beneficial to complete a more comprehensive assessment of your child's strengths on an annual basis, using the approaches in Chapter Four, *Identify*.

3. Environment

In a strengths-based approach, your child's environment is the first port of call for looking for ways to use and develop strengths. Identify resources in your child's environment that can be useful in terms of strengths use and development. Resources can refer to individuals, clubs/groups or institutions.

INDIVIDUALS

It may be strange to consider individuals in terms of the environment, and please be assured that individuals are discussed in this chapter in relational terms too. When thinking about an individual as a resource in your child's environment, it helps to think about what they can offer to cultivating a strengths-based approach with your child in terms of information, knowledge, strengths and time. For example, individuals in your child's environment may be very useful sources of information. This information could be in relation to your child's strengths and help in the identification of strengths. Individuals may have information on how to develop or use strengths. For example, your neighbour could know of a new music class starting that may be of interest to your child. If your child expresses the strength of love of learning, there may be an individual in your child's environment who has knowledge that may be highly interesting to your child. For example, if your child is creative and this is expressed in an interest in buildings, a local historian may well be a good person to make contact with. It can be very rewarding to connect with individuals in the environment that share strengths with your child. It is also helpful to think of people in the environment as potentially having the time to give to developing some of your child's strengths. Grandparents, aunts and uncles can often be so generous with their time, and you can count yourself and your child as fortunate if they are willing to give time to building your child's strengths.

CLUBS AND GROUPS

When you have an autistic child, it helps to think creatively about how groups and clubs in your child's environment can be used to support your child's strengths. For example, the sensory environment of our local Scouting club did not suit my son, however, he did attend some activities that helped develop strengths and skills in creativity and teamwork. Swimming lessons in our local leisure club did not suit my children – again, mainly for sensory reasons – but I was flexible and brought my children at a quieter time and taught them to swim quite quickly myself. This certainly helped develop perseverance in all of us. Increasingly, clubs are becoming more aware of neurodiversity, and many try to diminish their access barriers, accommodate needs and be inclusive in their approach.

What I have found helpful when my children attend clubs and groups is to make a passport document for the group leaders to read. Passports of this kind are not a new idea and have been used in education for decades. In my experience, there are a few guidelines that maximize the efficacy of a passport, including the following:

- Use first-person language.
- Include your child in the process.
- Use simple and clear language.
- Keep the passport to one page.
- Include a photograph.
- For child safety and GDPR (data protection) reasons, mark the passport as private and confidential, request that no copies are made and ask for the passport to be returned to you at the end of your child's involvement in the club/group.
- Keep the information to what will be very useful for the group leader to know.
- Please adapt the template to suit your child, for example,

medical and dietary needs, toilet and dressing support, if they are left-handed, if they have fears...

- If possible, laminate.

A passport template is included at the end of the chapter.

INSTITUTIONS

Being autistic, your child is likely to have interactions with more institutions than their neurotypical peers. Institutions have the potential to be a valuable resource when it comes to continued support of your child's strengths.

SCHOOL

School and the education system is an institution that your child is most likely to have regular interaction with. In recent times, there have been efforts to enhance social and emotional learning in schools, and supporting the strengths of all learners falls into the realm of social and emotional learning. Having an awareness of your child's strengths is so useful when meeting with your child's school and, in my experience, helps with advocacy. Asking your child's teacher and other school support workers to help to identify your child's strengths is one way to support your child using a strengths-based approach. Following on from this, there are several classroom and support-room-based resources that you could recommend to your child's school. These include Weaving Wellbeing (Rock and Forman 2016), which is a comprehensive whole-school positive-psychology programme. I have successfully adapted lessons in this programme to suit autistic pupils.

OUTSIDE AGENCIES

What outside agencies your child is involved with is dependent on several factors, including your child's access barriers and where you live. Outside agencies could possibly include CAMHS (Child and Adolescent Mental Health Services), regional autism services and associated health teams, often comprising psychologists, speech and language therapists and occupational therapists. If your child has regular involvement with these outside agencies, there may be scope to include them in a strengths-based approach with your child. When meeting a therapist or clinician, a passport (as outlined earlier) can be a very useful document, especially in the initial meeting. There is an alternative to the passport, called the All About Me sheet in Part Three of the book. Assessments that are carried out by professionals may uncover strengths, and the professionals may be able to provide specific recommendations for your child to develop their strengths further.

4. Resources

Consider what resources your child is likely to need to identify and use their strengths to their fullest potential, and use this as a starting point. Several factors will, of course, feed into identifying and procuring resources. Gathering resources does not necessarily mean spending vast sums of money. Having too many resources to use with autistic individuals can sometimes actually limit strength use. For example, creativity is one of my daughter's signature strengths and she has plenty of art materials. 1 find she is more creative if she only has a few resources to choose from. While researching this book, 1 was able to put my love of learning to good use, however, 1 found 1 maximized this strength if 1 focused on a smaller selection of research articles at any one time. Thinking about strengths in terms of resources can be very helpful if your extended family celebrate birthdays and holidays like Christmas. Knowing your child's strengths helps you and your relatives to be more selective in choosing gifts for your child.

5. Relationships

Relationships that build hope are considered vital in a strengths-based approach. A relationship that is built on acceptance and empathy is important. Relationships that help a child develop their strengths should increase the child's awareness of their abilities, increase the child's options in using their strengths and increase the child's opportunities to choose a strengths-based approach (Rapp 1998).

There are many relationships that will influence your child's life and help them identify, use and develop their strengths. This standard in the strengths-based approach has a significant overlap with resources and environment. In addition to relationships with siblings, extended family, friends and teachers, your autistic child is likely to have key relationships with support teachers, special needs assistants/teaching assistants, therapists and other support workers. It is useful to explore the nuances of these relationships with your child.

An exercise that can help identify relationships that will enhance the strengths-based approach is Circles of Influence. This is a popular coaching exercise and the variation I use here is adapted with permission from Nikki Giant (2014). It is useful to do this exercise at least annually. This exercise is especially helpful during periods of transition like the move from primary school to post-primary school.

CIRCLES OF INFLUENCE

AIMS

- To identify the people in the child/young person's life.
- To establish the individuals who are part of a support system for the child.
- To detect the people who can help the child use and develop their strengths.

METHOD

1. To begin this exercise, I would recommend using your child's strengths diary or a large blank page. If you prefer, please use the handout provided at the end of this chapter or simply use the handout as a guide. In any case, you will need three overlapping circles to complete this exercise.
2. This exercise will ideally be done with your child. If this is not possible, it is still a highly informative exercise to do by yourself.
3. In the top circle, write down all the people who are closest to them. Give your child as much help as they need with this.
4. In the next circle, fill in all the people who are next in terms of closeness. Typically, these include people who have a long-term relationship that is not as close as a direct family member, friends, family friends, extended family members and sometimes long-term tutors, teachers, therapists and childminders.
5. Complete the last circle with people who have less influence and/or a shorter-term impact on your child's life. It would be

expected to see classmates, teammates, friends they meet on holidays, shorter-term therapists, clinicians and school staff in this circle.

6. Using a highlighter, mark people who have been influential in identifying, exploring and developing your child's strengths.

These circles can help clarify what relationships are important to strengths development. For example, imagine your child has zest as a signature strength and they take swimming lessons for ten weeks. The swimming instructor is likely to be in the last circle as they are a short-term relationship in your child's life. However, it is probable that this relationship was a significant one in developing your child's strength.

6. Choice

Choice is a crucial standard in any strengths-based approach. Your child is far more likely to engage in identifying, exploring and developing their strengths if there is a strong element of meaningful choice built into the support you offer. Each child is an expert on their strengths, goals and hopes. It is your role as a parent providing support to help your child act upon their choices and encourage your child's efforts.

In Summary

▸ This chapter is the final chapter in the IDEAS Framework.

▸ This chapter explored sustaining support in using a strengths-based approach.

▸ We explored six standards of a strengths-based approach.

1. *Goals* – CO-OP approach, TATs, SMARTER framework and the miracle question.

2. *Assessment* – Review of the approaches in Chapter Three, *Identify*.

3. *Environment* – Individuals, clubs/groups and institutions.

4. *Resources* – Resources does not always mean a huge financial outlay. Sometimes, less is more with autistic individuals.

5. *Relationships* – Using the Circles of Influence approach.

6. *Choice* – Meaningful choice in strength use and development is a key factor in success with a strengths-based approach.

▸ Supporting worksheets based on the six standards of a strengths-based approach are included at the end of the chapter.

CIRCLES OF INFLUENCE[1]

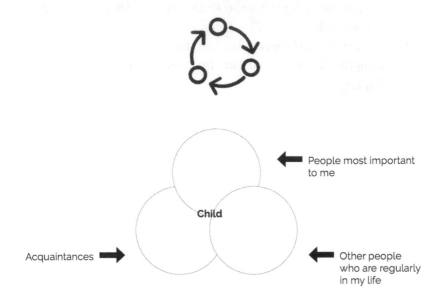

1. How can each group of people help identify my strengths?

2. How can each group of people help explore my strengths?

3. How can each group of people help use my strengths?

4. How can each group of people help develop my strengths?

---

1 The Circles of Influence worksheet from Giant, N. (2014) *Life Coaching for Kids: A Practical Manual to Coach Children and Young People to Success, Well-Being and Fulfilment.* London: Jessica Kingsley Publishers, is adapted with permission of the author.

MY PASSPORT

Insert photo here

Hi, my name is . . . .

I am . . . . years old.

I mainly communicate by . . . .

I have no medical conditions or allergies.

I go to . . . . school.

I know . . . . at camp.

My strengths are. . . . .

I am very frightened of. . . . .

You can help me by. . . . .

My emergency contacts are:

. . . .

Please return to my parents at the end of this group. Please do not photocopy. This information in my passport is private and confidential.

SETTING A GOAL USING THE SMARTER APPROACH

What is my goal? . . . .

    S Is it **s**pecific?

    M Can I **m**easure progress?

    A Is it **a**chievable?

    R Is it **r**ealistic?

    T Is it **t**imebound?

    E Can I **e**valuate progress?

    R Can I **r**eview if my goal is not going to plan?

After answering these questions, this is my goal broken down into steps:

Goal: . . . .

    Step 1: . . . .

    Step 2: . . . .

    Step 3: . . . .

    Step 4: . . . .

    Step 5: . . . .

PART THREE

Applying a Strengths-Based Approach

In Part Two, we learned about using the IDEAS Framework. Now, in Part Three, we consolidate what we have learned and focus on you, the parent, as we explore ways that we can apply the learning from Part One and Part Two. In Chapter Eight, we will discuss how you can apply the principles learned in the first two parts of the book to your own well-being and personal development. This involves us looking at applying a strengths-based approach to your life. We will look at self-coaching using the IDEAS Framework, and other effective coaching models. In Chapter Nine, we will explore a strengths-based approach to advocacy. We will look at an eight-step plan for successful advocacy, a stepped approach to advocacy for when your initial efforts are unsuccessful, advocacy and the neurodiversity movement, and self-advocacy.

CHAPTER EIGHT

A Strengths-Based Approach for Parents

By now, you have most likely taken some steps to think about, identify, explore and support your child's strengths. However, in this part of the book, I really want to shift the focus from your child to you, the parent. Taking a strengths-based approach is not only for children. Indeed, in my role as a coach, I devote time and effort to empowering adults to maximize their strengths in their daily life. In this chapter, I want to share some of the knowledge I have gathered about using a strengths-based approach with adults and in particular, parents of autistic children.

There is research into the wellbeing of parents who have autistic children, and some of it is quite difficult to read, especially when you are a parent to an autistic child. It is, however, more difficult to read as an autistic individual, as much of the research is negative in its focus towards autism. For example, a 2020 study demonstrated that having an autistic child was related to higher levels of parental stress and conflicts, which were, in turn, related to increased marital discord (Chan and Leung 2020). These findings highlight the importance of helping parents of autistic children manage stress and reduce conflicts (Chan and Leung 2020). These findings are consistent with other research projects (Alyoubi and Alofi 2020, Shorey *et al.* 2020). As a parent to two autistic children, I can say that there are challenges, but in my experience, the difficulty and challenge mainly lie in navigating support systems that are lacking in resources and having to advocate for what is right for my children. Rather than only focusing on what is difficult, I think it is far more helpful and more in the scope of the book to explore a strengths-based approach for parents.

Thankfully, not all the research feeds into a negative narrative. There have been some interesting studies into using a strengths-based approach with the parents of autistic children. One such study explored the character strength of gratitude in parents of autistic children. This 2018 study acknowledged gratitude as being associated with a greater sense of wellbeing in individuals generally. The researchers decided to study the use of gratitude as a PPI with mothers of autistic children for eight weeks. This intervention was conducted online, and wellbeing of the mothers was assessed pre and post intervention. The results were impressive in that the mothers experienced an increased sense of wellbeing, increased self-efficacy in their parenting, positive parenting characteristics and improved relationships (Timmons and Ekas 2018). This study suggests that by taking an interest in a character-strengths-based approach, parents of autistic children may be able to improve their wellbeing.

In another 2020 study, Zhao and Fu researched parents (of autistic children) who seemed to exhibit high levels of resilience. They found that character strengths of courage, hope and perseverance were very protective of the wellbeing of the parents studied. These character strengths seem to promote resilience. Resilience or bouncebackability after adversity can improve the problem-solving capability of parents and help them positively cope with stress (Berliner and Benard 1995). Furthermore, parents with high levels of resilience have fewer symptoms of depression and higher self-efficacy in their parenting (Pastor-Cerezuela *et al.* 2016). Indeed, this study emphasized that these character strengths of courage, hope and perseverance have an important stress buffer effect. The importance of supportive interventions to boost the wellbeing and resilience of parents of autistic children is also supported by a 2020 study that examined the efficacy of a mind-body intervention (Millstein *et al.* 2020). This intervention led to an improvement in resilience, stress and coping in parents of autistic children.

In my experience, PPIs have a positive effect on my wellbeing. I have a daily mindfulness practice; I am aware of my strengths and use them wisely and engage in regular coaching. Many of the autistic people that I coach are also parents to autistic children. Here, I would like to share some approaches that I use and know to be effective.

Self-Coaching Using Character Strengths

The first step I would encourage you to take if you are considering using PPIs to enhance your wellbeing is a character-strengths approach. The IDEAS Framework is not only suitable for children, it is also an ideal tool for adults to use for self-coaching. However, I would also like to share some other approaches with you. A key resource for adult character-strength coaching is the work of McQuaid, Niemiec and Doman (2018). They describe the eighty-twenty deficit bias, where we spend eighty percent of our time and effort fixing what is not working, leaving only twenty percent of our time and effort for what is working. By using a strengths-based approach, we have the opportunity to change the ratio to direct more of our precious time and effort into what is working well for us. Using our strengths helps us challenge our brain's natural negativity bias and helps us use our strengths to achieve our goals. By using our character strengths, we can access our other strengths, including our talents, skills and resources.

We have explored the advantages of a strengths-based approach, and McQuaid *et al.* summarize the research into strengths very nicely. For example, they remind us that using strengths leads to:

- increased wellbeing
- lower levels of stress
- better physical health
- increased life satisfaction
- increased confidence
- better performance at work.

With this information in mind, let us now look at using the IDEAS Framework for adult self-coaching.

Identify – Online Strengths-Identification Tools

The first step I would take in using a character-strength approach is completing an online strengths-identification survey. I would recommend the VIA Adult Survey. Time and time again, this is the survey that my adult coachees prefer and feel is most accurate. I also use the Cappfinity Strengths Profile, and coachees can find this useful if they are interested in exploring their career or career and study options. Both surveys use different strengths lists, and the VIA twenty-four-strength classification is what you will be most familiar with from reading this book. Any of the approaches outlined in Chapter Three, *Identify*, can also be used by an adult and will help form a more complete profile of your strengths.

Describe – Descriptions of your Character Strengths
The VIA website gives a short description of each strength and, of course, there is a child-centric description of each strength in this book. For those of you who would like more information on their signature strengths I would recommend the descriptions in: *Character Strengths and Virtues: A Handbook and Classification* (Seligman and Peterson 2004) or *Character Strengths Interventions: A Field Guide for Practitioners* (Niemiec 2017).

Explore
The ideas for exploring character strengths outlined in this book can also be applied to adults. Take time to think about people you admire and notice if you share any character strengths with them. The characters in books you read and movies you watch offer a rich source to explore your character strengths.

Action
All the recommendations in Chapter Six, *Action*, are suitable for an adult using character strengths to self-coach.

Support
In terms of support, the six standards of a strengths-based approach are as relevant to adults as they are to children.

GOALS
Goal setting using your strengths as an additional tool in your toolbox is highly effective for adults. Frameworks like the SMARTER approach are effective for adult goals too. For example, I consistently set goals while writing this book and broke them down further into TATs. The miracle question approach is one that I use myself and also with my adult coachees.

ASSESSMENT

This standard is explored fully in Chapter Three, *Identify*.

ENVIRONMENT

In Chapter Seven, *Support*, we discussed how individuals, clubs/groups and institutions can be helpful when taking a strengths-based approach with your child. These supports are also available to you in your environment. Individuals in your environment who might help you take a strengths-based approach might be close family members and friends who will help you identify and remind you of your strengths. Clubs and groups can be a hugely supportive element of your environment. It may be that you decide to join a group or a club to switch off from parenting for an hour a week. Joining a club or a group that also enables you to use your strengths would be advantageous. Many parents of autistic children join groups that aim to support and educate their members, and these groups, especially if run or advised by autistic people, can be hugely beneficial.

RESOURCES

It can be very beneficial to adequately resource your strengths-based approach. However, it is not always possible to invest significant financial and time resources into using and developing your strengths. For example, if you plan to increase your use of zest as a character strength, it may not be possible to devote resources to a significant fitness project like training for a triathlon or marathon. However, there is usually a scaled-back version of a plan that is realistic in terms of resources. Spending time at the goal-setting part of planning will ensure that resources are fully considered in your strengths-based approach.

RELATIONSHIPS

Sometimes, using a strengths-based approach can really help relationships. If you have a partner, being aware of each other's strengths can be helpful. If you take a strengths-based approach, you will most likely help build your relationship with your child, as there will be increased opportunity for you to model strength use and development for your child.

CHOICE

If you are self-coaching, it is already quite likely that there is a significant level of meaningful choice built into your approach. Choose approaches to strength use and development that excite you and have the potential to bring joy to your life.

Other Approaches for Adults

For the remainder of the chapter, I will outline some other approaches from coaching and positive psychology that are available to adults for a strengths-based approach. The IDEAS Framework is not the only coaching framework available to the individual who is interested in using their character strengths. Coaches and other professionals who use character strengths in their work with clients use a range of frameworks that suit a character-strengths approach.

GROW Model[1]

This coaching model is popular among coaches and leaders who take a coaching approach. Indeed, it is the first coaching model I learned to use, and I have integrated it successfully when taking a strengths-based approach to coaching adults. This model was developed by Sir John Whitmore in 1992. Since then, it has been used and adapted by many coaches and leaders, especially in the corporate world. In this model, **G** represents the goal. It is effective to describe the goal in as much detail as possible. **R** represents the reality of the current situation. This could be a reflection on how well you are using your strengths in the present moment or the reality of how you are using your strengths to reach a particular goal. Following this, **O** can represent obstacles that are in your way or opportunities that are available to you right now. Finally, **W** represents the way forward. This could be the plan that you are now going to implement using your strengths. **W** sometimes represents your will, that is, your motivation to act on the plan you have designed. There is a blank GROW Model grid at the end of this chapter that I find very useful when taking a strengths-based approach to goal setting.

---

1   Permission to use the GROW Model granted by The Estate of Sir John Whitmore and Performance Consultants International.

Appreciative Inquiry[2]

Gordon (2008) developed a framework based on appreciative inquiry (AI). This always proves very popular when I use it to coach adults using a strengths-based approach. This framework allows the individual to use their strengths by combining them with their past and imagined future. When self-coaching using this method, you will follow four steps (McQuaid *et al.* 2018).

DISCOVER

In this stage, you complete the VIA Survey and any of the strategies you would like to use as outlined in the Chapter Three, *Identify*.

DREAM

Use a strategy like the miracle question or imagining your best future self by writing what your life would be like in the future if you used your strengths to their fullest potential every day (King 2001).

DESIGN

At this stage, it is helpful to design what is called a hope map (Lopez 2013). This is an exercise where you write your goal and how you are going to use your strengths along the way to achieve that goal.

DELIVER

The final stage is using the strengths that you need to reach your goal until this becomes a habit. This process can be helped by completing an exercise called the strengths development habit (McQuaid and Lawn 2014). This is creating a simple plan to develop one of your strengths.

PERMA(H) Model

The PERMA(H) Model (Seligman 2012) is an ideal way to frame self-coaching. We explored this model in the opening chapters. Here, we will examine this model through the lens of self-coaching and look at

---

2   The Four Stepped AI method from McQuaid, M., Niemiec, R. and Doman, F. (2018) 'A character strengths-based approach to positive psychology coaching' In S. Green and S. Palmer (eds) *Positive Psychology Coaching in Practice*. London: Routledge. Adapted and reproduced with permission of the Licensor through PLSclear.

how it can help you develop a plan for a flourishing future (Falecki *et al.* 2018). If you would like to use PERMA(H) in self-coaching, I would recommend taking a pre-intervention assessment like the PERMA Profiler (Butler and Kern 2015) at the beginning of the process. At the end of the chapter, there is a handout that outlines PPIs that link to each pillar of the PERMA(H) Framework.

In Summary

- In this chapter, the focus shifted from your child to yourself.
- Research into the use of PPIs with parents of autistic children was discussed.
- Self-coaching was presented as a way of you taking a strengths-based approach to your own goal setting and wellbeing.
- Tips and information for using the IDEAS Framework to direct self-coaching were given.
- We explored other coaching models, including the GROW Model, an appreciative inquiry model and the PERMA(H) Framework.
- Handouts that help with the ideas discussed are included at the end of the chapter.

★

THE GROW MODEL[3]

	G	What is your goal?
	R	What is your current reality in terms of this goal?
	O	What are your options? What are your obstacles?
	W	What is the way forward? On a scale of 1–10, what is your will to try to reach this goal?

3   Adapted from Whitmore 1992. Permission to use the GROW Model granted by The Estate of Sir John Whitmore and Performance Consultants International.

APPRECIATIVE INQUIRY 4D COACHING MODEL[4]

Icon	Stage	Activity	Notes
	DISCOVER	VIA Survey – take the online VIA Survey.	
	DREAM	Best Possible Future Self Exercise (King 2001) Write about what might be possible if you used your strengths often to the best of your ability.	
	DESIGN	Hope Map Exercise (Lopez 2013) Write your goal and set pathways by writing down what strengths will help you reach your goal. Explain how they will help you reach your goal.	
	DELIVER	Strengths Development Habit Exercise (McQuaid and Lawn 2014) This uses the cue, routine and reward habit-making loop. Make a weekly timetable where you use an identified strength on an at least daily basis.	

---

4   The Four Stepped AI method from McQuaid, M., Niemiec, R. and Doman, F. (2018) 'A character strengths-based approach to positive psychology coaching.' In S. Green and S. Palmer (eds) *Positive Psychology Coaching in Practice.* London: Routledge. Adapted and reproduced with permission of the Licensor through PLSclear.

SELF-COACHING USING PERMA(H)

Icon	Pillar	PPIs	Notes
	POSITIVE EMOTIONS	• Gratitude journal • Savouring activities (including eating, smelling and observing) • Random acts of kindness (RAK) • Self-love meditation • Journaling • Read and/or watch Barbara Fredrickson's work on positive emotions	
	ENGAGEMENT	• Strengths identification, completing the VIA Survey • Finding flow activities	
	RELATIONSHIPS	• Sending thank-you notes	
	MEANING	• Exploring values • Goal setting • Positive CBT	
	ACCOMPLISH-MENT	• Yoga • Developing strengths • Positive affirmations • Exploring grit	
	HEALTH	• Following physical and mental health guidelines	

CHAPTER NINE

Advocacy Using a Strengths-Based Approach

Advocacy is when an individual or a representative for the individual acts to improve that person's life. It can be viewed as a form of 'a non-violent empowerment' (Munro 1991, p.1). Munro, an experienced service provider and clinician, believes that advocacy is effective when it succeeds in settling concerns and creates a climate where raising concerns is encouraged and seen as part of positive communication between the advocate and other party, usually a service provider. Advocacy is multifaceted and can take many forms, including:

- seeking information
- taking a solution-focused approach
- liaising with services, institutions and organizations to improve services and secure interventions
- speaking on behalf of an individual or group of individuals (Ewles, Clifford and Minnes 2014).

Munro thinks that families benefit from training in advocacy because there can be differing philosophies between the family and the service provider; these service providers are usually underfunded and under-resourced, and the limited resources might be more likely to go to families who advocate most effectively.

Parental Advocacy

As a parent to an autistic child you are most likely accustomed to advocating for your child. Knowing your child's strengths helps with effective advocacy, and building your child's strengths is a powerful way to lay the foundations for self-advocacy in the future. Advocating for your child is not always easy, and it can be particularly difficult not to have your emotions overtake you in an advocacy situation. Throughout the years, I have advocated for my children and pupils with a wide range of individuals and organizations. Even though I am fortunate to have training in advocacy, I have still sometimes asked a third party to step in to advocate for me and my family. Munro (1991) gathered what he learned from effective advocators and found that there were eight commonalities that I share here with his permission.

Be Polite

By being polite and avoiding overly aggressive behaviours, you are more likely to have individuals in the organization listen to your concerns and requests. Ultimately, strong and positive relationships with the services have more potential to help your family than fraught and conflict-driven relationships.

Know the System

This is easier said than done, but the more you understand the big picture of an organization, the more likely it is that you will identify the professionals in the system that are best able to help your family meet their goals.

Timing

Munro identifies timing as being very important in advocacy. As much as is possible, advocate when your energy is high, and advocate for an intervention before the need for that intervention is too high.

Use Your Strengths

If you are stronger in writing, advocate in writing. If you think you are persuasive in person, request a meeting. If you have a partner, share the advocacy tasks based on your strengths.

Groupwork

Advocacy does not have to be a lone process. Work with your family, your child's school or a professional that knows your child well.

Compromise

Be willing to compromise. As mentioned earlier, many services are under-resourced and underfunded. They may not be able to offer the intervention in the duration, frequency and intensity your child needs, but perhaps they can design and oversee a home programme that you can then implement.

The Human Story

Individualize your advocacy as much as possible. This could be an All About Me sheet prepared by your child, a voice note from your child stating what they need from the service or your child's list of strengths or strengths diary. When I did my advocacy training, it was recommended that I bring a photograph of my children along to advocacy meetings.

Show Appreciation

The professionals working in services usually want to help. If an individual has been helpful or provided effective intervention, it is important to show your appreciation through saying thank you, either verbally or in writing. On several occasions, I have advocated for my children with a professional, only for that professional to advocate for my children at another stage.

I know many of you will be very effective advocates, and for those of you who would like some more support, this is an eight-step approach that I hope you will find helpful. There is a planning grid at the end of the chapter to help you plan when advocating for your child.

Advocacy Using an Eight-Step Approach

1. **Goal(s)**
   - What is the goal of your advocacy?
   - What do you want to be different for your child as a result of your advocacy?

2. **Audience**
   - Who is it that you are approaching to make a change or a difference?
   - Try to ensure that you are contacting the most appropriate person in the organization for action to take place.
   - Is it best for the advocacy to come from you or a third party?
3. **Plan**
   - Create a plan using the CO-OP approach or SMARTER approach.
4. **Communicate**
   - Choose the best possible way to communicate with the person or organization you are presenting your plan to.
   - There may well be an accepted or established way to communicate.
   - Take into account your own communication preferences too, and make these explicit in your correspondence.
   - In this communication, your request and/or plan should be made clearly and backed up with evidence if appropriate.
   - Make sure that your goal is clearly stated in this communication.
5. **Create a plan**
   - If your advocacy has been successful, the next step is likely a meeting with the individual or organization.
   - In this meeting, agree on a plan. This will vary depending on what you are advocating for but is likely to contain:
     - goal(s)/targets/outcomes, both short term and long term
     - people involved
     - resources needed
     - timelines (may include appointments and assessments).
6. **Implement plan**
   - Implement your plan and give it enough time and effort to take effect.
7. **Evaluate**
   - Evaluate your initial plan and give and receive feedback from all parties involved.
8. **Next steps**
   - Identify the next steps, ideally collaboratively.

Even with a well-executed plan, advocacy is not always successful. Munro (1991) offers a stepped approach to escalating your advocacy efforts. These are shared as options and not as should dos. You will most likely know how much energy you have to invest in this advocacy. I have often backed down on advocacy, especially if I feel that my wellbeing or that of my family is suffering.

Munro's Stepped Approach (1991, p.5)[1]

1. Redefine your advocacy goal.
2. Develop your new plan.
3. Implement your plan.
4. If this attempt is unsuccessful, go to the next person in the service, usually a line manager.
5. If this is unsuccessful, gather supporters. These could be other parents, advocacy groups and politicians.
6. If still unsuccessful, go further. This will typically involve contacting senior figures in, and possibly outside, the service, for example, the Children's Ombudsman.
7. If all other attempts at this point have failed and the need is significant, this is the time to consider legal options.
8. Consider engaging with the media, including social media.
100. Non-violent protest. Munro calls this step one hundred to emphasize that this is a last resort.

The Neurodiversity Movement and Advocacy

There are some other important considerations when it comes to advocacy, whether it is a family member advocating on behalf of an autistic family member or an autistic individual who is self-advocating. Leadbitter *et al.* (2021) argue that advocates should have an understanding of the neurodiversity movement. This understanding involves knowing that autism is part of the natural variation found in humans and does not need to be cured or fixed in any way. Some important points that Leadbitter *et al.* (2021) raise include the following.

---

1   Reproduced here with permission from the original author.

- In advocacy, there should be a focus on the autistic individual's strengths and interests.
- The focus of advocacy should be on the real need for improving wellbeing and quality of life in autistic individuals.
- Language preferences should be respected.
- Interventions offered should be aligned with the needs of autistic people.
- There should be a respect and a recognition of autism as an essential aspect of the individual.
- Neurodiversity advocacy should include those who cannot advocate for themselves.
- An autistic individual can at once want to be themselves but want some aspects of their life to be different.
- Families and professionals need to avoid normative interventions that encourage masking.
- There is often a need to make environmental adaptations for autistic individuals.
- There is a need for the child's non-autistic peers to learn about neurodiversity.
- There is a need for families and professionals working with autistic children to have an awareness of a neurodivergent developmental trajectory.
- The priorities of the autistic individual should be taken into account when planning interventions and learning plans.
- The child should be able to say 'no'.

Self-Advocacy

By advocating for your child, you are modelling the process for them. Self-advocacy requires a wide range of skills that your child will hopefully build incrementally. They, like many other individuals, may need support in advocating for quite some time into the future, and this is okay too. I believe it is an asset to self-advocacy if a child has a good awareness of their strengths. There are several other factors that help self-advocacy. These include knowledge about autism diagnosis, awareness of communication preferences and an understanding of the neurodiversity movement.

Knowledge about Diagnosis

A child will have a more solid foundation for self-advocacy if they know about their diagnosis. Telling a child about their autism diagnosis is something that I am asked for advice on quite frequently. I was extremely fortunate to have two highly skilled and empathetic psychologists to guide me when I was having conversations with my children about their diagnoses. Here, I will share some general advice about talking to your child about their diagnosis. This is a personal and individualized area, and there is no one right way to share this information with your child.

GUIDELINES ON EXPLORING A DIAGNOSIS WITH YOUR CHILD

- Ideally, spend time reflecting on your understanding of your child's diagnosis before you talk to your child.
- Decide what language you will use. My preference is for identity-first language.
- Think about how you will describe autism. I described it as a difference rather that a condition or a disorder to my children.
- Try to anticipate the questions your child is likely to ask.
- Consider having examples of neurodivergent role models to hand.
- Approach telling your child about their diagnosis in terms of strengths and challenges. There is an example sheet on how to do this at the end of this chapter. On the sheet, list your child's strengths and talents and rate your child's strengths from +1 to +5 and their weaknesses from –1 to –5. Once you have this completed, you can explain to your child that when a person has strengths and challenges similar to theirs, it is possible that they have a difference known as autism.
- Exploring the strengths and challenges of family members, as well as a sheet of their strengths and challenges, can be very comforting for your child. You may want to use the sheet at the end of the chapter.

Communication Preferences

Your child's communication preferences may change over time. In self-advocacy, it is important that the child is encouraged to use the communication style that they prefer. It may be that your child uses augmentative and alternative communication (AAC). Whatever way your child communicates should be accommodated when they are self-advocating. One way a child can use non-verbal communication to self-advocate is to share an All About Me sheet when they are engaging with a service. This can be completed with you in advance. It allows your child to use their voice when planning an intervention and brings them into the centre of the process. This sheet can be adapted and could include information like strengths, communication preferences, and supports and adaptations that will help during the intervention.

An Understanding of the Neurodiversity Movement

It is helpful for autistic children to have some knowledge of the neurodiversity movement. How much they need to know will depend on several factors. Neurodiversity is not a simple topic, and learning about it can happen over the course of years. It may be appropriate for older children and adolescents to have more information about the neurodiversity movement. There is a child-friendly factsheet on neurodiversity at the end of the chapter. If your child is interested in the topic, it would be beneficial to mind map the topic with them.

In Summary

▸ In this chapter, we looked at a strengths-based approach to advocacy.

▸ Advocacy is described as 'a non-violent empowerment' (Munro 1991, p.1).

▸ We explored successful parental advocacy, including advice from Munro (1991), an eight-step planning guide and a stepped approach when you are unsuccessful in your advocacy efforts.

▸ We looked at how the neurodiversity movement shapes advocacy.

▸ The concept of self-advocacy was introduced, with knowledge of diagnosis, awareness of communication preferences and an understanding of neurodiversity being identified as important foundations of self-advocacy.

▸ Some worksheets are shared at the end of the chapter.

ADVOCACY USING AN EIGHT-STEP APPROACH

Icon	Step	Your notes
	GOAL(S)	
	AUDIENCE	
	PLAN	
	COMMUNICATE	
	CREATE A PLAN	
	IMPLEMENT	
	EVALUATE	
	NEXT STEPS	

MY STRENGTHS AND CHALLENGES

Strengths and challenges	Busy and noisy places	Meeting new people	Change	Learning about new things	Swimming	Honesty	Wearing new and scratchy clothes	Focusing on interesting work	Perseverance
+5									
+4									
+3									
+2									
+1									
-1									
-2									
-3									
-4									
-5									

This is an example of a completed Strengths and Challenges worksheet. I did not limit myself to character strengths when completing this sheet, as I wanted to demonstrate that a flexible approach with this sheet is best. You may find other ways of presenting this information visually. Please use whatever approach you think will work best for your child. It can be very helpful and comforting for children if a worksheet is completed for other family members, as it makes it more explicit that everyone has strengths and challenges.

MY STRENGTHS AND CHALLENGES

+5									
+4									
+3									
+2									
+1									
Strengths and challenges									
-1									
-2									
-3									
-4									
-5									

ALL ABOUT ME

Insert photo here (optional)

Hi, my name is . . . .

I am . . . . years old.

I mainly communicate by . . . .

I prefer to use . . . . first language.

My strengths are . . . .

My interests are . . . .

You can help me by . . . .

By the end of this intervention, this is what I would like to be different.

. . . .

. . . .

. . . .

Other information I think you should know about me:

. . . .

. . . .

. . . .

Please do not photocopy. This information is private and confidential.

NEURODIVERSITY

- The term *neurodiversity* was invented by an Australian lady called Judy Singer in the late 1990s.
- Neurodiversity is like biodiversity, and just like there is a wide variety of life on the planet, there are also different types of brains.
- Some brains are described as neurodivergent and some are described as neurotypical.
- High-tech brain scans are starting to show us differences in the way the brain and the nervous system are wired.
- The neurodiversity movement teaches us that people who have neurodivergent brains do not need to be cured or fixed.
- Being neurodivergent can often mean that that individual has different experiences, perhaps in their environment, with communication and with their senses. Changing someone's environment can often be helpful for any individual but especially a neurodivergent individual.
- There are neurodivergent people in all types of careers and activities.
- The more someone knows about their neurotype, the more likely they are to understand themselves.

CHAPTER TEN

Conclusion

Throughout this book, we have been on a journey together, exploring your child's strengths and learning how you can help your child discover, develop and apply their character strengths. It is my sincere wish that you found this book useful and that you will reread sections and share what you have learned with others. After the references, I have included suggestions for further reading and reviewing. The research articles and books that I have referenced are in the reference section.

I want to re-emphasize that it is not necessary to complete every exercise in this book. Please pick and choose the activities that you think will be most beneficial to your child. Activities that do not seem relevant now may well be of use in the future.

I do hope that you will take some time to consider the self-coaching activities in Chapter Eight. They really do help support self-care; this is so important for everyone but particularly for busy parents with many demands on their time.

Finally, Chapter Nine, about advocacy, demonstrates how an awareness of strengths can be applied to real-life situations. Using strengths in advocacy has the potential to be powerful for your child.

I have very much enjoyed sharing my experiences with you over the course of the book. I have certainly used my strengths in new and sometimes unexpected ways throughout the research and writing process. I wish you and your child every success while using this book and hope that you find it a fun and rewarding experience!

In Summary

▸ This brief chapter concludes the book and the exploration of the IDEAS Framework and is followed by a list of references, further reading recommendations and a brief section explaining some terms used throughout the book.

References

Abeler, J., Falk, A. and Kosse, F. (2021) 'Malleability of preferences for honesty.' *CESifo Working Paper* No. 9033. Accessed on 15/07/21 at SSRN: https://ssrn.com/abstract=3832488.

Adler, A. (1963) *Individual Psychology*. Paterson, NJ: Littlefield: Adams & Company.

Agius, J. and Levey, S. (2019) 'Humour and autism spectrum disorders.' Accessed on 15/07/21 at www.um.edu.mt/library/oar/handle/123456789/45461.

Alyoubi, R. A. and Alofi, E. A. (2020) 'Experiences of parenting child with ASD during COVID-19 pandemic: A cross-sectional study.' *Medical Science*, 3972–3980.

American Psychiatric Association (2013) *Diagnostic and Statistical Manual of Mental Disorders (DSM-5®)*. San Francisco, CA: American Psychiatric Publications.

Attwood, T. and Gray, C. (1999) 'The discovery of "Aspie" criteria.' *The Morning News, 11*(3).

Baltes, P. B. and Staudinger, U. M. (2000) 'Wisdom: A metaheuristic (pragmatic) to orchestrate mind and virtue toward excellence.' *American Psychologist, 55*(1), 122.

Bandura, A. (1997) *Self-Efficacy: The Exercise of Control*. New York: W. H. Freeman.

Baron-Cohen, S., Ring, H. A., Wheelwright, S., Bullmore, E. T., Brammer, M. J., Simmons, A. and Williams, S. C. (1999) 'Social intelligence in the normal and autistic brain: An fMRI study.' *European Journal of Neuroscience, 11*(6), 1891–1898.

Beardon, L. (2007) 'Is autism a disorder?' *No. 1 in the ARM UK Need to know series*. Accessed on 15/07/21 at https://blogs.shu.ac.uk/autism/2018/07/17/is-autism-a-disorder.

Berliner, B. A. and Benard, B. (1995) 'More than a message of hope: A district-level policymaker's guide to understanding resiliency.' Portland, OR: Western Regional Center for Drug-Free Schools and Communities.

Bharath, S. (2017) 'Build zest and create a positive institution for children to learn.' Accessed on 15/07/21 at https://medium.com/@SharanyaBharath/build-zest-and-create-a-positive-institution-for-children-to-learn-fb7484630f12.

Blankenship, K. L. and Whitley, B. E. (2000) 'Relation of general deviance to academic dishonesty.' *Ethics & Behavior, 10*(1), 1–12.

Birmingham, C. (2010) 'Romance and irony, personal and academic: How mothers of children with autism defend goodness and express hope.' *Narrative Inquiry, 20*(2), 225–245.

Biswas-Diener, R., Kashdan, T. B. and Minhas, G. (2011) 'A dynamic approach to psychological strength development and intervention.' *The Journal of Positive Psychology, 6*(2), 106–118.

Bogdashina, O. (2013) *Autism and Spirituality: Psyche, Self, and Spirit in People on the Autism Spectrum*. London: Jessica Kingsley Publishers.

Boniwell, I. (2008) *Positive Psychology in a Nutshell: A Balanced Introduction to the Science of Optimal Functioning*. London: Personal Well-Being Centre.

Botha, M., Hanlon, J. and Williams, G. L. (2021) 'Does language matter? Identity-first versus person-first language use in autism research: A response to Vivanti.' *Journal of Autism and Developmental Disorders*.

Brooks, R. and Goldstein, S. (2013) 'Changing the mindset of children and adolescents with autism spectrum disorders.' *Interventions for Autism Spectrum Disorders: Translating Science into Practice, 325*.

Brown, J. and Wong, J. (2017) 'How gratitude changes you and your brain.' Accessed on 15/07/21 at https://greatergood.berkeley.edu/article/item/how_gratitude_changes_you_and_your_brain.

Brunstein, J. C. (1993) 'Personal goals and subjective well-being: A longitudinal study.' *Journal of Personality and Social Psychology, 65*(5), 1061.

Buckingham, M. (2007) *Go Put Your Strengths to Work: 6 Powerful Steps to Achieve Outstanding Performance.* London: Simon and Schuster.

Burnett, N. and Thorsborne, M. (2015) *Restorative Practice and Special Needs: A Practical Guide to Working Restoratively with Young People.* London: Jessica Kingsley Publishers.

Butler, J. and Kern, M. L. (2015) *The PERMA Profiler.* Philadelphia, PA: University of Pennsylvania.

Buzan, T. (2005) *Mind Maps for Kids.* London: Thorsons.

Casey, W. M. and Burton, R.V. (1982) 'Training children to be consistently honest through verbal self-instructions.' *Child Development,* 911–919.

Chan, K. K. S. and Leung, D. C. K. (2020) 'The impact of child autistic symptoms on parental marital relationship: Parenting and coparenting processes as mediating mechanisms.' *Autism Research, 13*(9), 1516–1526.

Cohen, S., Doyle, W. J., Turner, R. B., Alper, C. M. and Skoner, D. P. (2003) 'Emotional style and susceptibility to the common cold.' *Psychosomatic Medicine, 65*(4), 652–657.

Colby, A. and Damon, W. (2010) *Some Do Care.* New York: Simon and Schuster.

Cosden, M., Koegel, L. K., Koegel, R. L., Greenwell, A. and Klein, E. (2006) 'Strength-based assessment for children with autism spectrum disorders.' *Research and Practice for Persons with Severe Disabilities, 31*(2), 134–143.

Cost, K. T., Zaidman-Zait, A., Mirenda, P., Duku, E., Zwaigenbaum, L., Smith, I. M. and Vaillancourt, T. (2021) '"Best things": Parents describe their children with autism spectrum disorder over time.' *Journal of Autism and Developmental Disorders,* 1–15.

Coulson, J. (2021) 'The three free things every kid needs from their parents.' Accessed on 08/07/22 at www.kidspot.com.au/parenting/dr-justin-coulson-the-three-free-things-every-kid-needs-from-their-parents/news-story/f0c3e8540bd4a1fb3aa48e61f8ed9aab.

Covey, M. K., Saladin, S. and Killen, P. J. (2001) 'Self-monitoring, surveillance, and incentive effects on cheating.' *Journal of Social Psychology, 129,* 673–679.

Csikszentmihalyi, M. (1978) 'Intrinsic rewards and emergent motivation.' In M. R. Lepper and D. Greene (eds) *The Hidden Costs of Reward: New Perspectives on the Psychology of Human Motivation.* New York: Erlbaum.

Csikszentmihalyi, M. and Seligman, M. E. (2000) 'Positive psychology: An introduction.' *American Psychologist, 55*(1), 5–14.

Deci, E. L. and Ryan, R. M. (2000) 'The "what" and "why" of goal pursuits: Human needs and the self-determination of behavior.' *Psychological Inquiry, 11*(4), 227–268.

de Schipper, E., Mahdi, S., de Vries, P., Granlund, M., Holtmann, M., Karande, S. and Bölte, S. (2016) 'Functioning and disability in autism spectrum disorder: A worldwide survey of experts.' *Autism Research, 9*(9), 959–969.

Dillenburger, K., Röttgers, H. R., Dounavi, K., Sparkman, C., Keenan, M., Thyer, B. and Nikopoulos, C. (2014) 'Multidisciplinary teamwork in autism: Can one size fit all?' *The Educational and Developmental Psychologist, 31*(2), 97–112.

Dowling, J. S. (2014) 'School-age children talking about humour: Data from focus groups.' *International Journal of Humour Research, 27*(1), 121–139.

Duckworth, A. L., Peterson, C., Matthews, M. D. and Kelly, D. R. (2007) 'Grit: perseverance and passion for long-term goals.' *Journal of Personality and Social Psychology, 92*(6), 1087.

Dweck, C. (2006) *Mindset: How We Can Learn to Fulfil Our Potential.* New York: Random.

Dweck, C. S. (2012) 'Mindsets and human nature: Promoting change in the Middle East, the schoolyard, the racial divide, and willpower.' *American Psychologist, 67*(8), 614.

Dweck, C. (2015) 'Carol Dweck revisits the growth mindset.' *Education Week, 35*(5), 20–24.

Dweck, C. (2016) 'What having a "growth mindset" actually means.' *Harvard Business Review, 13,* 213–226.

Dweck, C. S. (2017a) 'The journey to children's mindsets—and beyond.' *Child Development Perspectives, 11*(2), 139–144.

Dweck, C. (2017b) *Mindset-Updated Edition: Changing the Way You Think to Fulfil Your Potential*. New York: Hachette.

Dykshoorn, K. L. and Cormier, D. C. (2019) 'Autism spectrum disorder research: Time for positive psychology.' *Autism Open Access*, 9(1).

Ekas, N. V., Pruitt, M. M. and McKay, E. (2016) 'Hope, social relations, and depressive symptoms in mothers of children with autism spectrum disorder.' *Research in Autism Spectrum Disorders*, 29, 8–18.

Ewles, G., Clifford, T. and Minnes, P. (2014) 'Predictors of advocacy in parents of children with autism spectrum disorders.' *Journal on Developmental Disabilities*, 20(1), 73.

Falecki, D., Leach, C. and Green, S. (2018) 'PERMA-Powered Coaching: Building Foundations for a Flourishing Life.' In S. Green and S. Palmer (eds) *Positive Psychology Coaching in Practice*. London: Routledge.

Faulkner, G., Hefferon, K. and Mutrie, N. (2015) 'Putting positive psychology into motion through physical activity.' *Positive Psychology In Practice*, 2, 207–222.

Fowler, J. H. and Christakis, N. A. (2008) 'Dynamic spread of happiness in a large social network: Longitudinal analysis over 20 years in the Framingham Heart Study.' *BMJ*, 337.

Fredrickson, B. L. (1998) 'What good are positive emotions?' *Review of General Psychology*, 2(3), 300–319.

Fredrickson, B. L. (2001) 'The role of positive emotions in positive psychology: The broaden-and-build theory of positive emotions.' *American Psychologist*, 56(3), 218.

Fredrickson, B.L. (2006) *Positivity*. New York: Three Rivers Press.

Fredrickson, B.L. and Levenson, R. (1998) 'The question: "Does religion (or spirituality) cause physical health benefits?"' *Journal of Personality and Social Psychology*, 5(4), 432–443.

Fredrickson, B. L., Tugade, M. M., Waugh, C. E. and Larkin, G. R. (2003) 'What good are positive emotions in crisis? A prospective study of resilience and emotions following the terrorist attacks on the United States on September 11th, 2001.' *Journal of Personality and Social Psychology*, 84(2), 365.

Furlong, M. J., Gilman, R. and Huebner, E. S. (2014) 'Enhancing Well-Being in Youth: Positive Psychology Interventions for Education in Britain.' In M.J. Furlong, R. Gilman and E.S. Huebner (eds) *Handbook of Positive Psychology in Schools*. London: Routledge.

Gable, S. L., Reis, H. T., Impett, E. A. and Asher, E. R. (2018) 'What do you do when things go right? The intrapersonal and interpersonal benefits of sharing positive events.' In H.T. Reis (ed.) *Relationships, Well Being and Behaviour*. Abingdon and New York: Routledge

Gander, F., Proyer, R. T., Ruch, W. and Wyss, T. (2013) 'Strength-based positive interventions: Further evidence for their potential in enhancing well-being and alleviating depression.' *Journal of Happiness Studies*, 14(4), 1241–1259.

Gardner, H. (1983) *The Theory of Multiple Intelligences*. Portsmouth, NH: Heinemann.

Garland, E. L., Fredrickson, B., Kring, A. M., Johnson, D. P., Meyer, P. S. and Penn, D. L. (2010) 'Upward spirals of positive emotions counter downward spirals of negativity: Insights from the broaden-and-build theory and affective neuroscience on the treatment of emotion dysfunctions and deficits in psychopathology.' *Clinical Psychology Review*, 30(7), 849–864.

Gebhardt, M., Schwab, S., Krammer, M. and Gegenfurtner, A. (2015) 'General and special education teachers' perceptions of teamwork in inclusive classrooms at elementary and secondary schools.' *Journal for Educational Research Online*, 7(2), 129–146.

Giant, N. (2014) *Life Coaching for Kids: A Practical Manual to Coach Children and Young People to Success, Well-Being and Fulfilment*.' London: Jessica Kingsley Publishers.

Gilar-Corbí, R., Pozo-Rico, T., Sánchez, B. and Castejón, J. L. (2018) 'Can emotional competence be taught in higher education? A randomized experimental study of an emotional intelligence training program using a multimethodological approach.' *Frontiers in Psychology*, 9, 1039.

Goleman, D. (2012) *Social Intelligence: The New Science of Human Relationships*. London: Bantam.

Gordon, S. (2008) 'Appreciative inquiry coaching.' *International Coaching Psychology Review*, 3(1), 17–29.

Green, L. S., Oades, L. G. and Robinson, P. L. (2012). 'Positive psychology and coaching psychology in schools.' In C. van Nieuwerburgh (ed) *Coaching in Education: Getting Better Results for Students, Educators, and Parents.* London: Karnac.

Hammond, W. (2010) 'Principles of strength-based practice.' *Resiliency Initiatives, 12*(2), 1–7.

Harter, J. K., Schmidt, F. L. and Keyes, C. L. (2003) *Well-being in the Workplace and its Relationship to Business Outcomes: A Review of the Gallup Studies.* Accessed on 15/07/21 at http://media.gallup.com/DOCUMENTS/whitePaper--Well-BeingInTheWorkplace.pdf.

Hartley, C. and Fisher, S. (2018) 'Do children with autism spectrum disorder share fairly and reciprocally?' *Journal of Autism and Developmental Disorders, 48,* 2714–2726.

Harzer, C. and Ruch, W. (2014) 'The role of character strengths for task performance job dedication, interpersonal facilitation, and organizational support.' *Human Performance, 27*(3), 183–205.

Held, B. S. (2004) 'The negative side of positive psychology.' *Journal of Humanistic Psychology, 44*(1), 9–46.

Hill, P. C. and Sandage, S. J. (2016) 'The promising but challenging case of humility as a positive psychology virtue.' *Journal of Moral Education, 45*(2), 132–146.

Hills, K., Clapton, J. and Dorsett, P. (2019) 'Spirituality in the context of nonverbal autism: Practical and theological considerations.' *Practical Theology, 12*(2), 186–197.

Kashdan, T. B. and Fincham, F. D. (2002) 'Facilitating creativity by regulating curiosity.' *American Psychologist, 57*(5), 373–374.

King, L. A. (2001) 'The health benefits of writing about life goals.' *Personality and Social Psychology Bulletin, 27*(7), 798–807.

Kirchner, J., Ruch, W. and Dziobek, I. (2016) 'Brief report: Character strengths in adults with autism spectrum disorder without intellectual impairment.' *Journal of Autism and Developmental Disorders, 46*(10), 3330–3337.

Krapp, A. and Fink, B. (1992) 'The Development and Function of Interests During the Critical Transition from Home to Preschool.' In K.A. Renninger, S. Hidi, A. Krapp and K. Renninger (eds) *The Role of Interest in Learning and Development.* New York: Psychology Press.

Laurent, A. C. and Gorman, K. (2018) 'Development of emotion self-regulation among young children with autism spectrum disorders: The role of parents.' *Journal of Autism and Developmental Disorders, 48*(4).

Lavy, S. and Littman-Ovadia, H. (2011) 'All you need is love. Strengths mediate the negative associations between attachment orientations and life satisfaction.' *Personality and Individual Differences, 50*(7), 1050–1055.

Leadbitter, K., Buckle, K. L., Ellis, C. and Dekker, M. (2021) 'Autistic self-advocacy and the neurodiversity movement: Implications for autism early intervention research and practice.' *Frontiers in Psychology, 12,* 782.

Lemon, J. M., Gargaro, B., Enticott, P. G. and Rinehart, N. J. (2011) 'Brief report: Executive functioning in autism spectrum disorders: A gender comparison of response inhibition.' *Journal of Autism and Developmental Disorders, 41*(3), 352–356.

Lewis, A. (2009) 'Methodological issues in exploring the ideas of children with autism concerning self and spirituality.' *Journal of Religion, Disability and Health, 13*(1), 64–76.

Licinio, J. (2016) 'PERMA: Positive emotion, engagement, relationships, meaning and accomplishment optimism, physical activity, nutrition, and sleep.' *Australia: South Australian Health and Medical Research Institute (SAHMRI), 10.*

Linley, A., Nielson, K. M., Wood, A. M., Gillet, R., and Biswas-Diener, R. (2010) 'Strengths and goals: Using signature strengths in pursuit of goals: effects on goal progress, need satisfaction, and well-being, and implications for coaching psychologists.' *International Coaching Psychology Review,* March.

Linley, P. A., Woolston, L. and Biswas-Diener, R. (2009) 'Strengths coaching with leaders.' *International Coaching Psychology Review, 4*(1), 37–48.

Lopez, S. J. (2013) *Making Hope Happen: Create the Future You Want for Yourself and Others.* New York: Simon and Schuster.

Lyons, V. and Fitzgerald, M. (2004) 'Humour in autism and Asperger syndrome.' *Journal of Autism and Developmental Disorders, 34*(5), 521–531.

Marks, N. A., Cordon, C., Aked, J. and Thompson, S. (2008) 'Five ways to wellbeing.' *New Economics Foundation*, 1–23.

Martin, R. A. (2007) *The Psychology of Humour: An Integrative Approach*. Burlington, MA: Elsevier Academic Press.

Martínez-Martí, M. L., Hernández-Lloreda, M. J. and Avia, M. D. (2016) 'Appreciation of beauty and excellence: Relationship with personality, prosociality and well-being.' *Journal of Happiness Studies*, *17*(6), 2613–2634.

McCabe, D. L. (1992) 'The influence of situational ethics on cheating among college students.' *Sociological Inquiry*, *62*(3), 365–374.

McCashen, W. (2005) *The Strengths Approach: A Strength-Based Resource for Sharing Power and Creating Change*. Bendigo, VIC: St Luke's Innovative Resources.

McCluskey, G., Lloyd, G., Kane, J., Riddell, S., Stead, J. and Weedon, E. (2008) 'Can restorative practices in schools make a difference?' *Educational Review*, *60*(4), 405–417.

McDermott, D. and Hastings, S. (2000) 'Children: Raising future hopes.' In C.R. Snyder (ed.) *Handbook of Hope: Theory, Measures, and Applications*. San Diego, CA: Academic Press.

McKnight, P. E. and Kashdan, T. B. (2009) 'Purpose in life as a system that creates and sustains health and well-being: An integrative, testable theory.' *Review of General Psychology*, *13*(3).

McQuaid, M. and Lawn, E. (2014) *Your Strengths Blueprint: How to Be Engaged, Energized and Happy at Work*. Australia: Michelle McQuaid Pty Ltd.

McQuaid, M., Niemiec, R. and Doman, F. (2018) 'A character strengths-based approach to positive psychology coaching.' In S. Green and S. Palmer (eds) *Positive Psychology Coaching in Practice*. London: Routledge.

Memisevic, H. and Pasalic, A. (2021) 'Executive functions and developmental profiles in preschool children with autism spectrum disorder.' Accessed on 15/07/21 at https://europepmc.org/article/PPR/PPR313652.

Millstein, R. A., Lindly, O. J., Luberto, C. M., Perez, G. K., Schwartz, G. N., Kuhlthau, K. and Park, E. R. (2020) 'An exploration of health behaviors in a mind-body resilience intervention for parents of children with developmental disabilities.' *Journal of Developmental and Behavioral Pediatrics: JDBP*, *41*(6), 480.

Milton, D. E. (2012) 'On the ontological status of autism: The "double empathy problem".' *Disability and Society*, *27*(6), 883–887.

Munro, J. D. (1991) 'Training families in the "Step Approach Model" for effective advocacy.' *Canada's Mental Health*, *39*, 1–6.

Murray, D., Lesser, M. and Lawson, W. (2005) 'Attention, monotropism and the diagnostic criteria for autism.' *Autism*, *9*(2), 139–156.

Mutrie, N. and Faulkner, G. (2004) 'Physical Activity: Positive Psychology In Motion.' *Positive Psychology In Practice*, 146–164.

Niemiec, R. M. (2017) *Character Strengths Interventions: A Field Guide for Practitioners*. Boston, MA: Hogrefe Publishing.

Niemiec, R. M., Shogren, K. A. and Wehmeyer, M. L. (2017) 'Character strengths and intellectual and developmental disability: A strengths-based approach from positive psychology.' *Education and Training in Autism and Developmental Disabilities*, *52*(1), 13–25.

Otake, K., Shimai, S., Tanaka-Matsumi, J., Otsui, K. and Fredrickson, B. L. (2006) 'Happy people become happier through kindness: A counting kindnesses intervention.' *Journal of Happiness Studies*, *7*(3), 361–375.

Owens, B. P., Johnson, M. D. and Mitchell, T. R. (2013) 'Expressed humility in organizations: Implications for performance, teams, and leadership.' *Organization Science*, *24*, 1517–1538.

Park, N. and Peterson, C. (2005) 'The values in action inventory of character strengths for youth.' In K. Anderson Moore and L.H. Lippmann (eds) *What Do Children Need to Flourish?* Boston, MA: Springer.

Park, N. and Peterson, C. (2006) 'Values in Action (VIA) Inventory of Character Strengths for Youth.' *Adolescent and Family Health*, *4*(1), 35–40.

Park, N. and Peterson, C. (2009) 'Character strengths: Research and practice.' *Journal of College and Character*, *10*(4), 1–10.

Pastor-Cerezuela, G., Fernández-Andrés, M. I., Tárraga-Mínguez, R. and Navarro-Peña, J. M. (2016) 'Parental stress and ASD: Relationship with autism symptom severity, IQ, and resilience.' *Focus on Autism and Other Developmental Disabilities, 31*, 300–311.

Pasupathi, M., Staudinger, U. M. and Baltes, P. B. (2001) 'Seeds of wisdom: Adolescents' knowledge and judgment about difficult life problems.' *Developmental Psychology, 37*(3), 351.

Pearson, A., Rees, J. and Rose, K. (2022) '"I felt like I deserved it because I was Autistic": Understanding the impact of interpersonal victimisation in the lives of autistic people.' *Autism*, June.

Perry, B. D. and Hambrick, E. P. (2008) 'The Neurosequential Model of Therapeutics.' *Reclaiming Children and Youth, 17*(3), 38–43.

Peterson, C. and Seligman, M. E. (2004) *Character Strengths and Virtues: A Handbook and Classification* (Vol. 1). New York: Oxford University Press.

Polatajko, H. and Mandich, A. (2004) *Enabling Occupation in Children: The CO-OP Approach.* Nepean, ON: Canadian Association of Occupational Therapists.

Prizant, B. M. and Fields-Meyer, T. (2015) *Uniquely Human: A Different Way of Seeing Autism.* New York: Simon and Schuster.

Purkis, Y. (2017) '"Take me to your leader" – Autism and leadership.' Spectrum Women. Accessed on 15/07/21 at www.spectrumwomen.com/featured/take-me-to-your-leader-autism-and-leadership-by-jeanette-purkis.

Quirici, M. (2015) 'Geniuses without imagination.' *Journal of Literary and Cultural Disability Studies, 9*(1), 71–89.

Rapp, C. A. (1998) *The Strengths Model: Case Management with People Suffering from Severe and Persistent Mental Illness.* New York: Oxford University Press.

Rapp, C. A., Saleebey, D. and Sullivan, W. P. (2006) 'The future of strengths-based social work.' *Advances in Social Work: Special Issue on the Futures of Social Work, 6*(1), 79–90.

Rezaei, A. and Jeddi, E. M. (2020) 'Relationship between wisdom, perceived control of states, perceived stress, social intelligence, information processing styles and life satisfaction among college students.' *Current Psychology, 39*(3), 927–933.

Riosa, P. B., Chan, V., Maughan, A., Stables, V., Albaum, C. and Weiss, J. A. (2017) 'Remediating deficits or increasing strengths in autism spectrum disorder research: A content analysis.' *Advances in Neurodevelopmental Disorders, 1*(3), 113–121.

Roche, M. (2020) 'Critical thinking and book talk: An approach to developing critical thinking abilities in the early years.' Accessed on 08/07/22 at https://thesector.com.au/2020/07/01/critical-thinking-and-book-talk-an-approach-to-developing-critical-thinking-abilities-in-the-early-years

Rock, M. and Forman, F. (2016) *Weaving Well-Being Programme.* Dublin: Outside the Box Learning Resources Ltd.

Rogé, B. and Mullet, E. (2011) 'Blame and forgiveness judgements among children, adolescents, and adults with autism.' *Autism, 15*(6), 702–712.

Ruch, W. (2001) 'The perception of humor.' In A. Kaszniak (ed.) *Emotions, Qualia, and Consciousness.*

Ruch, W. and Köhler, G. (1998) 'A Temperament Approach to Humor.' *The Sense of Humor: Explorations of a Personality Characteristic*, 203–230.

Salimi, A., Abbasi, A., Zahrakar, K., Tameh, B. and Davarniya, R. (2017) 'The effect of group-based hope therapy on resiliency of mothers of children with autism spectrum disorder.' *Armaghane Danesh, 22*(3), 350–363.

Santos, I. and Groves, D. (2021) 'Filled and Unfulfilled Hope: The Effect of Imagery on Self-Regulatory Resources and Emotion.' *20th Annual Celebration of Undergraduate Research and Creative Activity*, Paper 6.

Scarantino, L. (2020) 'Being brave with autism.' *Autism Parenting Magazine. 93: ASD Advice for Today and Tomorrow.*

Scarnati, J. T. (1997) 'Beyond technical competence: Honesty and integrity.' *Career Development International, 2*(1), 4.

Schmidt, L., Kirchner, J., Strunz, S., Broźus, J., Ritter, K., Roepke, S. and Dziobek, I. (2015) 'Psychosocial functioning and life satisfaction in adults with autism spectrum disorder without intellectual impairment.' *Journal of Clinical Psychology, 71*(12), 1259–1268.

Scott, T. M. (2020) 'Phenomenological study on the persistence of autism spectrum disorder students in college.' *Doctoral Dissertation.* Phoenix, AZ: Grand Canyon University.

Seligman, M. E. (2012) *Flourish: A Visionary New Understanding of Happiness and Well-Being.* Boston, MA: Simon and Schuster.

Seligman, M. E., Steen, T. A., Park, N. and Peterson, C. (2005) 'Positive psychology progress: Empirical validation of interventions.' *American Psychologist, 60*(5), 410.

Seymour, K. and Wise, P. (2017) 'Circus training for autistic children: Difference, creativity, and community.' *New Theatre Quarterly, 33*(1), 78–90.

Sheldon, K. M. and Houser-Marko, L. (2001) 'Self-concordance, goal attainment, and the pursuit of happiness: Can there be an upward spiral?' *Journal of Personality and Social Psychology, 80*(1), 152.

Sheldon, K. M. and Lyubomirsky, S. (2007) 'Is it possible to become happier? (And if so, how?).' *Social and Personality Psychology Compass, 1*(1), 129–145.

Shorey, S., Ng, E. D., Haugan, G. and Law, E. (2020) 'The parenting experiences and needs of Asian primary caregivers of children with autism: A meta-synthesis.' *Autism, 24*(3), 591–604.

Smith, J., Staudinger, U. M. and Baltes, P. B. (1994) 'Occupational settings facilitating wisdom-related knowledge: The sample case of clinical psychologists.' *Journal of Consulting and Clinical Psychology, 62*(5), 989.

Taggart, G. (2015) 'Sustaining care: Cultivating mindful practice in early years professional development.' *Early Years, 35*(4), 381–393.

Tanksale, R., Sofronoff, K., Sheffield, J. and Gilmour, J. (2021) 'Evaluating the effects of a yoga-based program integrated with third-wave cognitive behavioral therapy components on self-regulation in children on the autism spectrum: A pilot randomized controlled trial.' *Autism, 25*(4), 995–1008.

Testoni, I., Pesci, S., De Vincenzo, C., Dal Corso, L. and Zamperini, A. (2019) 'Work and spirituality among people with Asperger syndrome: An exploratory study.' *Journal of Disability and Religion, 23*(2), 178–196.

Timmons, L. and Ekas, N. V. (2018) 'Giving thanks: Findings from a gratitude intervention with mothers of children with autism spectrum disorder.' *Research in Autism Spectrum Disorders, 49*, 13–24.

Torske, T., Nærland, T., Øie, M. G., Stenberg, N. and Andreassen, O. A. (2018) 'Metacognitive aspects of executive function are highly associated with social functioning on parent-rated measures in children with autism spectrum disorder.' *Frontiers in Behavioral Neuroscience, 11*, 258.

Tugade, M. M. and Fredrickson, B. L. (2004) 'Resilient individuals use positive emotions to bounce back from negative emotional experiences.' *Journal of Personality and Social Psychology, 86*(2), 320.

Valle, M. F., Huebner, E. S. and Suldo, S. M. (2004) 'Further evaluation of the Children's Hope Scale.' *Journal of Psychoeducational Assessment, 22*(4), 320–337.

Van Eylen, L., Boets, B., Steyaert, J., Wagemans, J. and Noens, I. (2015) 'Executive functioning in autism spectrum disorder: Influence of task and sample characteristics and relation to symptom severity.' *European Child and Adolescent Psychiatry, 24*(11), 1399–1417.

Van Willigen, M. (2000) 'Differential benefits of volunteering across the life course.' *The Journals of Gerontology Series B: Psychological Sciences and Social Sciences, 55*(5), S308–S318.

Walker, P. (2013) *Complex PTSD: From Surviving to Thriving.* Scotts Valley, CA: Create Space Publishing.

Waters, L. and Loton, D. (2019) 'SEARCH: A meta-framework and review of the field of positive education.' *International Journal of Applied Positive Psychology, 4*(1), 1–46.

Watts, R. E. (2013) 'Reflecting as if.' *Counseling Today, 55*(10), 48–53.

White, E. R., Hoffmann, B., Hoch, H and Taylor, B. A. (2011) 'Teaching teamwork to adolescents with autism: The cooperative use of activity schedules.' *Behavior Analysis in Practice, 4*(1), 27–35.

Whitmore, J. (1992) *Coaching for Performance: A Practical Guide to Growing Your Own Skills.* Nicholas Brealey Publishing.

Whitmore, J. and Performance Consultants International (2017) *Coaching for Performance. The principles and practice of coaching and leadership.* Nicholas Brealey Publishing.

Wolters, C. A. and Hussain, M. (2015) 'Investigating grit and its relations with college students' self-regulated learning and academic achievement.' *Metacognition and Learning,* 10(3), 293–311.

Wood, R. (2021) 'Autism, intense interests, and support in school: From wasted efforts to shared understanding.' *Educational Review,* 73(1), 34–54.

Worsley, R. (2020) 'What does autistic leadership look like in 2020?' Accessed on 09/06/22 at www.neurodiversitymedia.com/resource-library/what-does-autistic-leadership-look-like-in-2020.

Worthington Jr., E. L., Goldstein, L., Hammock, B., Griffin, B. J. *et al.* (2015) 'Humility: A qualitative review.' In C. N. Snyder, S. J. Lopez, L. M. Edwards and S. C. Marques (eds) *The Oxford Handbook of Positive Psychology, 3rd Edition.* New York: Oxford University Press Inc.

Xu, J. and Roberts, R. E. (2010) 'The power of positive emotions: It's a matter of life or death—Subjective well-being and longevity over 28 years in a general population.' *Health Psychology,* 29(1), 9.

Zager, D. (2013) 'Positive psychology and autism spectrum disorders.' In M. L. Wehmeyer (ed.) *The Oxford Handbook of Positive Psychology and Disability.* Oxford: Oxford University Press.

Zhao, M. and Fu, W. (2020) 'The resilience of parents who have children with autism spectrum disorder in China: A social culture perspective.' *International Journal of Developmental Disabilities,* 1–12.

Further Reading

Boniwell, I. (2012) *Positive Psychology in a Nutshell: The Science of Happiness*. Milton Keynes: Open University Press.

This book gives an easy-to-read yet comprehensive overview of positive psychology.

Honeybourne, V. (2017) *A Practical Guide to Happiness in Children and Teens on the Autism Spectrum: A Positive Psychology Approach*. London: Jessica Kingsley Publishers.

This book is written with professionals working with autistic children and teens in mind. It is, nevertheless a very useful resource for anyone interested in using PPIs with autistic children and young people.

Kantor, A., Lipsitt, L., Woodard, C. R. and Groden, J. (2011) *How Everyone on the Autism Spectrum, Young and Old Can...: Become Resilient, Be More Optimistic, Enjoy Humour, Be Kind, and Increase Self-Efficacy: A Positive Psychology Approach*. Philadelphia, CA: Jessica Kingsley Publishers.

I have had this book many years now. It gives a very comprehensive view of positive psychology and gives plenty of suggestions on developing resilience, optimism, humour and kindness. This book also includes an assessment called the ASPeCT Scale that would be beneficial for someone who is interested in assessing their child's progress. The activities are perhaps more suited to parents and professionals who take a behaviouralist approach in their interventions. They can, of course, be adapted.

Roberts, F. and Wright, E. (2020) *Character Toolkit: Strength Cards*. London: Jessica Kingsley Publishers.

These are very attractively illustrated cards that, although not exactly aligned with the VIA character strengths, would be very useful for the activities in Chapter Three of this book, *Identify*.

Wheeler, M. (2020) *Getting Started: Introducing Your Child to His or Her Diagnosis of an Autism Spectrum Disorder*. Accessed 16/07/21 at www.iidc.indiana.edu/irca/learn-about-autism/getting-started-introducing-your-child-to-his-or-her-diagnosis-of-autism.html.

This is short guide that will give you ideas on how to explore an autism diagnosis with your child. Wheeler has a comprehensive list of resources, including picture books, for you to draw from.

Terms Used in This Book

There may be some terms that are new to you as you read this book. I have selected terms that are not used in everyday speech and included them with a brief explanation here. Please take these explanations as a starting point. Some of the terms are complex and the brief explanation offered here is in no way presented as a complete and comprehensive exploration of the term. I have given references where there is direct further reading available.

Ableism
Ableism is a form of discrimination against disabled people. It can be overt or subtle. On a basic level, a building only providing stairs and not providing ramps and lifts is ableist. Functioning labels like high functioning and low functioning are also considered ableist.

Advocacy
Advocacy has several different meanings, but in the context of this book, it is when someone (the advocate) takes action to have the needs and rights of an individual met, often by a third party. The advocate works with this third party, keeping the needs and rights of the individual they are advocating for at the forefront of all discussions and decisions made about the individual.

Coaching
Coaching is another term that has several meanings. In the context of this book, coaching is a process that helps an individual reach their full potential through a series of conversations between a coach and a coachee. Throughout the book, several suggestions are given on how you as a parent can act as a coach for your child.

Double Empathy Problem (Milton 2012)
This is a theory by Damian Milton that describes why autistic and non-autistic people sometimes find it difficult to understand each other. It helps us recognize that breakdowns in understanding happen for both the autistic and non-autistic person, and therefore both parties have to make an effort if they want to understand

each other better. This is a significant theory and has important implications for interventions for autistic people, especially social skills training. This theory highlights the need for autistic and non-autistic people to understand that they have different communication styles.

Executive Functioning (EF)

Executive functioning is a group of mental processes that occur in the prefrontal cortex of the brain. The processes are linked to everyday tasks and learning and include organization, attention, regulation, and starting, doing and completing tasks. EF skills often benefit from support in autistic individuals.

Fawning (Walker 2013)

Fawning looks like people pleasing and avoiding conflict. It can be linked to trauma, and autistic masking and camouflaging. It is a response that is receiving increasing attention from the autism community.

Grit (Duckworth *et al.* 2007)

Grit is when someone uses perseverance to work hard towards their goals, even when it is difficult to do so. Grit is an important virtue in positive psychology and is linked to success and happiness.

Identity-First Language (Botha, Hanlon and Williams 2021)

Identity-first language is the preferred language use of the majority of the autism community (Botha *et al.* 2021). If I say, 'I am autistic,' I am recognizing autism as part of my identity and an integral part of me.

Info-Dumping

In relation to this book, info-dumping is a term used by the neurodivergent community to describe when someone, usually a neurodivergent individual, 'dumps' a large volume of fact about a topic. Info-dumping can bring huge satisfaction and enjoyment to the individual, as the subject of the info-dump is often the individual's particular interest.

Interoception

Interoception is a sensory system that helps us understand our internal states and physical sensations, like our heartbeat, hunger, pain, temperature and appetite. It also helps us interpret emotions.

Masking

Masking is a very complex phenomenon that is associated with autistic people. It is usually masking one's authentic autistic self to pass as neurotypical. This can include reducing and hiding stimming and appearing more extroverted than what is natural for the individual. Masking can be conscious and unconscious. Masking can be detrimental to the individual's mental health and wellbeing. Camouflaging, passing and covering are all related to masking.

Person-First Language (Botha *et al.* 2021)

Person-first language is if I referred to myself as a 'person with autism'. Person-first language is preferred by the minority of the autism community, and my personal preference is for identity-first language. However, many autism professionals use person-first language. When communicating with an autistic person, it is a good idea to check their language preferences.

Positive Psychology

Positive psychology is a field of psychology that focuses on what helps humans flourish and live good and meaningfully engaged lives.

Positive Education

Positive education is the application of positive psychology methods in a school or educational institution.

Self-Advocacy

When an individual self-advocates effectively, they are aware of their strengths and challenges. They can set goals and can communicate what they need in terms of supports and resources to achieve their goals.

Self-Efficacy (Bandura 1997)

Self-efficacy is an individual's belief that they have the power to achieve their goal and overcome challenges. It is linked to many positive outcomes including increased wellbeing and life satisfaction.

Self-Regulation

Self-regulation refers to a range of processes that are linked to self-control and self-awareness. Self-regulation can be challenging for autistic individuals; one reason for this is that our neurology is different to neurotypical neurology. This means we have to work harder to regulate our senses in some environments. Emotional regulation can also be difficult, partially due to EF and interoception differences.

Stim

Stim or stimming is an abbreviation for self-stimulatory behaviours. Everybody stims; for example, yawning, foot-tapping, knuckle cracking and lip biting are all forms of stimming. Stimming is very important to many autistic people, and we stim for many different reasons, including self-soothing, regulating, communicating and expressing emotions.